THE
M^cMICHAEL
CANADIAN
COLLECTION

KLEINBURG · ONTARIO

The Tom Thomson Shack

The McMichael Canadian Collection

KLEINBURG · ONTARIO

A Commentary by D. G. Carmichael, Canadian Journalist

Miracles aren't supposed to happen anymore. We live in an age of doubt and cynicism, and there simply is not room for anything that cannot be run through a computer terminal. The exception is the McMichael Canadian Collection at Kleinburg, Ontario. It is a miracle. It happened because of Robert and Signe McMichael, and the artists, patrons and government leaders to whom they sold their dream of a Canadian collection in a Canadian setting.

Only twenty-five years have gone by since Bob McMichael was a struggling young Toronto businessman and he and Signe were buying their first painting — Lawren Harris's *Montreal River* — from a Toronto art dealer on time payments of fifty dollars a month for five months.

From that humble beginning, the McMichael Collection has grown into a national treasure containing more than fifteen hundred paintings, prints and sculptures worth perhaps fifteen million dollars, but irreplaceable at any price, a treasure whose nucleus is the largest collection of Group of Seven paintings displayed anywhere.

But numbers are only half the story. The other half is how the McMichaels developed and won acceptance for the idea of a gallery that would show Canadian art in its own surroundings. Their collection, they decided, would be set in a massive log cabin of contemporary design whose windows would look out on the fields and woods like those that Canada's most beloved artists had painted. The paintings, they decided, would be hung not against plaster walls, but against a background of log, brick and barnboard. And later, after they had donated their original collection to the Province of Ontario, the same concept was continued in additions to their original home.

Probably some traditionalists scoffed at the idea, just as traditionalists had scoffed at the Group of Seven twenty-five or thirty years earlier when they had broken away from academic European painting techniques to form their own unique school. But the McMichaels stuck to their guns, and before long their idea began to attract support from the surviving members of the Group of Seven and from friends of Canadian art. As word of their collection spread, more and more people began arriving at the front door asking to see the paintings. By the early sixties, the McMichaels realized that the collection had grown far beyond their original expectations and that a way had to be found to maintain and display it, not only for the present but for future generations.

In 1964 the McMichaels invited to dinner the Premier of Ontario, John Robarts, and proposed a plan to him. They wished to donate to the Province their collection, their home and their property; in return the Province would assume responsibility for the safekeeping and maintenance of the paintings and grounds in perpetuity. It took Premier Robarts and his staff a year to work out the necessary legal machinery. In 1965, an agreement was signed transferring the collection and the property to the Province. The McMichaels would stay on as resident curators and the Province would maintain the gallery, staff it with guides and guards, and provide additional facilities for the public.

At the time of the agreement, the Collection consisted of about three hundred paintings by the Group of Seven, Tom Thomson and their contemporaries, including Emily Carr and David Milne. It has since been broadened to include Indian and Eskimo prints, sculptures and paintings, as well as work from a wider selection of artists. But the heart of the Collection, then as now, was the work of the Group and Thomson, now numbering more than five hundred paintings by Group members and over eighty by Thomson, the man many consider the greatest Canadian artist.

Although Thomson was not a member of the Group — he drowned in a canoe accident in Algonquin Park in 1917, three years before the Group was founded — his life and death had a profound effect on the men who were to become Group members, all of whom had known him, some of whom had worked with him, and a few of whom had been his closest friends.

As the McMichaels' collection grew, their own circle of acquaintances began to grow. An early meeting with one of the original members of the Group, Arthur Lismer, led to meetings with other members — A.Y. Jackson, A.J. Casson, Lawren Harris, Edwin Holgate, and Frederick Horsman Varley — and with other leading Canadian artists including Yvonne McKague Housser, Barker Fairley and Thoreau MacDonald, the son of original Group member J.E.H. MacDonald, who died in 1932.

The McMichaels began to receive donations of paintings from people who believed in what they were doing. At the time the McMichaels presented their collection to the Province in 1965, about three quarters of it had been purchased by them and the remainder had been donated. Today the figures are reversed — about three quarters of the Collection has been donated. The dependence of the Collection on lovers of Canadian art has been one of its strong points and is no accident. The McMichaels specifically asked that the Province not provide government grants for acquisitions.

Although the Collection does not have an acquisition budget as such, profits from the gift shop and donations are used to acquire works of art in cases where purchase is necessary and desirable. Not all possessors of works are wealthy, and in many cases in which a painting may be a person's insurance against financial difficulty, the owner is encouraged to sell the work to the Collection. On the other hand, many of the paintings in the Collection could not have been purchased at any price. They belonged to people to whom they meant more than money.

An early donor was Mrs. Norah de Pencier, of Leith, Ontario, near Owen Sound. Years before the Group became popular, she often invested half her modest salary as a book store manager in Canadian art. In the early sixties, she gave to the McMichaels Emily Carr's *Shoreline*, A.Y. Jackson's *Grey Day*, *Laurentians*, and four Tom Thomson sketches.

Financier R.A. Laidlaw presented twenty-six paintings to the Collection, including nine brilliant Tom Thomson sketches. Dr. A.D.A. Mason, dean of dentistry at the University of Toronto and friend to several members of the Group, gave *Leaves In The Brook*, one of J.E.H. MacDonald's greatest masterpieces. Noted Canadian artist Yvonne McKague Housser whose husband, the late F.B. Housser, wrote *A Canadian Art Movement*, a prime reference work on the Group, gave paintings by Harris, Jackson, Lismer and Carr. Industrialist Percy Hilborn of Preston, Ontario donated the magnificent A.Y. Jackson canvas *First Snow, Algoma*, which, of all the paintings Jackson produced, was the artist's favourite. In 1968, C.A.G. Matthews, who had employed both Frank Carmichael and A.J. Casson at Sampson Matthews Limited, gave a collection that had been carefully acquired over many years. S. Walter Stewart, a devotee of the Group since his days as a reporter on the University of Toronto *Varsity*, gave a collection of thirty A.Y. Jackson paintings, including *Red Maple*, that became the core of the Collection's Jackson holdings. R.S. McLaughlin, the automaker, in 1968 gave the most important part of his art collection to the McMichaels, including magnificent works by Clarence Gagnon, Maurice Cullen, J.W. Morrice and Emily Carr, as well as several monumental canvases by members of the Group.

In 1976 industrialist Garfield Weston, hearing that one of the last full-size paintings by Tom Thomson in private hands was about to be sold, quietly offered the Collection more than a quarter of a million dollars to purchase it.

No one knows how many paintings and sketches the Group produced — its members did not keep painting diaries, but it would be in the many thousands. McMichael once asked A.Y. Jackson how many paintings he had painted in his lifetime and Jackson told him he honestly had no idea. But one day a young boy trailing Jackson through the galleries asked him the same question and Jackson replied mischieviously "A million."

Jackson, like the other Group members, painted his field sketches on small wood panels, and if they failed to please him, he used the panels over again or tossed them into the fireplace.

McMichael says that although the paintings in the Collection represent a small part of the Group's output, they are among the very best in terms of quality. He explains that most of the Group paintings in the Collection were handpicked by the artists or by people who knew their work well. Lawren Harris, for instance, brought Tom Thomson's work to the attention of his friend Robert Laidlaw and A.Y. Jacskon helped Colonel McLaughlin when McLaughlin was developing his collection. And the McMichaels, of course, because of the intensive study they put into the Group's work, were able to select fine works themselves.

As their interest deepened, the McMichaels spent more and more time researching Canadian art and Canadian artists. Their collection of written material began to grow, and today the Collection's library and archives contain more than ten thousand items, including books, catalogues, photographs and letters by Canadian painters and writers, that form an important source of reference material. The McMichaels gradually became not only devotees of Canadian art, but experts in it. Ironically the interest their work attracted in the Group of Seven and other Canadian painters began to work against them in the marketplace, as it contributed to the prices of Canadian paintings skyrocketing in a decade.

The McMichaels do not know if there was an exact moment when they decided to donate their collection to the country, but they agree that their 1957 purchase of the hauntingly beautiful Tom Thomson winter scene *Afternoon, Algonquin Park*, was a turning point in the development of the Collection. It was one of the few larger Thomson canvases in private hands and when they took possession of it, they knew they had acquired not just a painting, but something that in a very real sense was a national treasure.

Bob and Signe's interest in Canadian art has always included the work of Indian and Eskimo artists. They acquired their first Eskimo carving in the early fifties and in 1956 acquired their first Northwest Coast Indian piece, an impressive Kwakiutl Raven Hamatsa mask.

The McMichaels have always believed that Northwest Coast Indian and contemporary Eskimo art is vital and unmistakably Canadian. Canada's Northwest Coast Indians had created a civilization whose images are recognized in most parts of the world. The Germans, British, Americans and others made early penetrations to the West Coast and recognized the importance of Indian masks and totems. Canadians came in late on an acceptance that was made by European collectors as early as the mid-1800's.

In 1976, the McMichael Collection established the first permanent exhibition area for Woodland Indian paintings. Traditionally, depicting their legends was taboo and regarded as an intrusion into beliefs considered sacrosanct by the people. However, Norval Morrisseau, an Ojibwa, persisted in developing a contemporary style of painting to interpret the life and legends of his people, and his early work inspired other Woodland Indian artists.

Because the McMichaels are, by nature, modest and retiring, many of the visitors to the Collection have the idea that after donating their collection to the Province in 1965, the McMichaels quietly faded away. Nothing could be further from the truth. The Collection's management and development are an all-consuming career and passion for both of them. And yet they stay very much in the background at Kleinburg, content to do their work behind the scenes. McMichael, wearing an old sweater and comfortable slacks moves through the galleries unnoticed and occasionally hears visitors discussing him. There is considerable fascination about the source of his wealth. Many visitors have the idea he made his money on the stock market or inherited it. In fact, McMichael made his money with an idea, and the hard work and merchandising ability required to exploit it.

After service with the Royal Canadian Navy in the Second World War, McMichael established a photographic studio in Toronto's Yorkville district. To advertise the studio, he got the idea of putting together a kit of manufacturers' samples and distributing them through newspapers, industries and retailers. As the business grew, McMichael spent less and less time on the photography, and more on the merchandising end. He expanded the business throughout the United States and for several years, he commuted weekly between Kleinburg and New York. In 1965 he sold the business to devote all his time to the Collection.

Such is McMichael's low profile in the galleries that recently a guide came rushing up to politely but firmly inform him that "Sir, you mustn't touch the paintings." McMichael had been discussing a painting with a writer and had gently lifted the painting to see if he could read the date beneath the artist's signature. When the guide realized it was McMichael, they both began to laugh, and McMichael sheepishly said: "I'm sorry. I won't do it again."

McMichael and his wife often think back to the days when Group of Seven sketches and paintings could have been bought easily for what now seems the proverbial song. In one art dealer's gallery they used to visit, Group of Seven paintings literally were stacked up against the wall and selling for prices that by today's standards would be laughable. In those days, however, says McMichael, he and his wife were trying to do three things — expand their collection, expand their business, and build a home — so there was a tight limit on the amount of money they could spend on paintings. In spite of this, they managed to accumulate the foundation of today's public collection.

Robert and Signe always have believed that there should not be any barrier between the Collection and the people who want to see and enjoy it. Although a box is provided for donations, the McMichaels and the Board of Trustees feel that no admission fee should be charged so that people can come as often as they like and bring their whole families.

The galleries are staffed with guides who know the background of the Collection and enjoy discussing it with visitors. Gallery education guides conduct tours for people of all ages. Mornings are reserved for school class tours, and almost 70,000 students visit the galleries annually. Because the floors are carpeted, students can sit on the floor, campfire style, while guides discuss the paintings and answer their questions. Many of these students return on weekends and during school holidays to introduce their parents and friends to an experience they obviously enjoyed.

An eloquent tribute to the spirit of the gallery is the special place the Collection has held in the affections of the artists whose work is exhibited in it. Varley and Holgate were frequent visitors to the gallery and became personal friends of the McMichaels. A.J. Casson has played an intimate role in the

Collection since its inception and designs its publications, as has Thoreau MacDonald, whose sketches illustrate this text. A.Y. Jackson chose to live with the McMichaels for the last six years of his life and virtually became the Collection's *curator emeritus*. People loved Jackson and a familiar sight was Alex, a gaggle of visitors in tow, moving through the galleries discussing the paintings.

Perhaps nothing better illustrates the character of the man than an incident that took place in the early sixties. Dr. Mason, mentioned earlier as the donor of MacDonald's great work *Leaves in the Brook*, had recently given the painting to the Collection. A short while later, Jackson came to lunch carrying a paper bag. In it was the panel for *Leaves in the Brook*. When MacDonald died, he had willed one sketch to each of the members of the Group and *Leaves* was the sketch he had willed to Jackson. Now Jackson wanted the McMichaels to have it.

The backgrounds of the McMichaels provide a clue to their affection for Canadian art. Signe's parents emigrated to Canada from Denmark when she was six, and she spent her formative years on the family farm in the Peace River district. Bob, though born in Toronto, has vivid recollections of summer visits to Algonquin Park and the Temagami area of northern Ontario. They saw in the work of the Group and its contemporaries the same love for the Canadian landscape that they felt themselves.

Their original home, *Tapawingo*, Indian for *Place of Joy*, was built on a ten-acre site on the outskirts of Kleinburg, then a hamlet of about two hundred people twenty miles northwest of Toronto. Friends doubted the wisdom of building a home so far from the city in an area that lacked city services and might be difficult for commuting in the winter. But in the intervening years, major highways have closed the gap. Fortunately for the Collection, however, the original property is enclosed in a vast green belt that makes it a natural haven from the stress of the city. Visitors to the Collection constantly are delighted by the number and variety of birds that visit the feeders outside the windows and the densely wooded property is a habitat for foxes, lynxes, raccoons, wolves, rabbits and deer.

During the two years before Tapawingo was built, the McMichaels scoured the countryside searching for old buildings to get timbers and barnboard for their "cabin". Timbers weren't as difficult to obtain in those days, and negotiations occasionally took an unusual twist. One old farmer said to Bob: "Let's get this straight. Do I pay you twenty-five dollars for taking my barn away or do you pay me?"

The dimensions of Tapawingo, though impressive in their day, have long since been dwarfed by the additions. Each main room of the original building had the same floor area as the average five-room house, and the walls were constructed from square-hewn logs nine inches thick. Amazingly, because of the massive fieldstone fireplaces, the rugs Signe chose for the floors, and the paintings on the walls, the rooms had a warmth and coziness rarely found in rooms of conventional size.

By retaining the original concept and employing the same local craftsmen who built the original home, the Collection has been able to maintain that warmth in the massive additions that have been built in the intervening years.

In 1962, a small but unique building was moved to the property. It was the shack in which Tom Thomson had lived and painted in Toronto's Rosedale Ravine, behind the Group of Seven's Studio Building. It has been furnished almost exactly as Thoreau MacDonald and A.Y. Jackson remembered it in 1915. Its walls are decorated with paintings by members of the Group and others, and there is a series of witty contemporary impressions of Group members by Arthur Lismer. Here also, are Thomson's easel and palette.

A touching moment occurred in 1974, when the last living member of Thomson's immediate family, his sister, Margaret Tweedale, then ninety, donated her collection of works by her brother.

In 1967, the Ontario Government approved a large new wing for the Collection and by the time it was opened in 1968, new acquisitions virtually filled its walls. In 1969, to provide additional galleries for the rapidly growing collection, ground was broken for another much larger wing, which contains two of the largest gallery rooms in the complex. One of these, the West Coast Gallery, contains more than three thousand square feet of floor space. It was constructed of huge Douglas fir logs from British Columbia, a fitting material for a showplace of art from a part of Canada where nature exists on such a vast scale.

The peaked roof soars to accommodate a Kwakiutl totem pole which is an example of the McMichaels' determination to achieve what many considered impossible. August, 1970 saw the McMichaels heading into the British Columbia wilderness in search of an original totem which might have survived the elements. Experts believed such a pole could not be found as the totems had long since been removed to museums or had deteriorated in the open beyond rescue. By good fortune, Robert and Signe found what they were looking for at Blunden Harbour, a totally deserted coastal island many miles off the rugged northern tip of Vancouver Island. In the nearby forest, they came upon the white pole surrounded by dark green cedars. After considerable negotiations, they purchased the pole which was carved by the great Kwakiutl artist Willie Seaweed, from his family and with the approval of the local band council.

Early ceremonial masks of the native Indian tribes of the West Coast peer down from the walls, the powerful Emily Carr canvases thrust forward views of mountains, forests, coastlines and Indian villages. In the centre of the room, is a huge bench, thirty-nine feet long by three feet wide, carved from a single red cedar log — a bench so large that two classes of school children can sit on it at one time.

On display here are magnificent examples of the works of the great Haida carver Bill Reid, two rare bracelets and five miniature totems by the master 19th century Haida carver Charles Edenshaw. The collection of early masks, many of magnificent quality, represent the Haida, Kwakiutl, Bella Coola, Bella Bella, Nootka, Salish, Tsimshian and Tlingit Indians. But perhaps the most awesome feature of the gallery is a huge carved figure whose shoulder once supported the roof of an Indian ceremonial house. He stands and glowers atop a legendary bear devouring a mischievous child.

Among the outstanding Emily Carr paintings in this gallery are those which were donated by Dr. and Mrs. Max Stern of Montreal and Dr. and Mrs. Murray Speirs of Toronto.

Adjoining the West Coast Gallery is another gallery of almost the same size, and in it are hung some of the most majestic works of the Group of Seven, works that demand a gallery of impressive proportions.

To accommodate the increasing number of visitors, a new entrance complex was opened in 1973. The huge structure whose centerpiece is an illuminated waterfall twenty-seven feet high, is used as an assembly point. Because of the size and number of the galleries, there never is need for lineups, even on the busiest days. The McMichaels planned the entrance complex to be symbolic of Canada. Outside the front door, facing directly north, is a polar bear sculpture by the Eskimo artist Pauta. On the west wall, inside the building, is a magnificent ancient longhouse entrance post from the Bella Coola Indians. Facing it on the east wall is an ancient anchor salvaged from Halifax harbour. And through the windows of the south wall the rolling hills and valleys of southern Ontario unfold.

When the Collection was given to the people of Canada in 1965, it was called the McMichael Conservation Collection and was administered through a small advisory committee. In 1972, Premier William Davis introduced legislation changing its name to the McMichael Canadian Collection and making its direction the responsibility of a nine-member board of trustees, serving without remuneration, appointed by the Cabinet and reporting to the Minister of Culture and Recreation.

Between August, 1976, and June, 1978, the McMichael Collection, which began with a young couple and a dream, became an ambassador for Canada abroad. An exhibition of forty-four paintings from the Collection was shown in Glasgow, Edinburgh, Aberdeen, London, Washington, Hamburg, Bonn, Munich, Oslo and Dublin, and in Russia at the Hermitage in Leningrad, the Museum of Western and Eastern Art in Kiev and the Pushkin Museum in Moscow. Between the time the tour began and the time it ended at the centuries-old Irish castle in Kilkenny, McMichael travelled more than 100,000 miles to represent the Collection and Canada at the various openings, and whenever possible, Signe accompanied him. Conducted under the auspices of the External Affairs Department of Canada and the Ontario Government, it was Canada's longest and most extensive cultural tour and catalogues were designed and printed in German, Russian and Norwegian as well as in English and French. Indeed the Collection had come a long way since Robert and Signe McMichael purchased Lawren Harris's *Montreal River* for $250 on time payments less than twenty-five years earlier.

In the hallway of their original home, *Tapawingo*, which is now part of a gallery, there is a barnboard carved with a quotation from a speech by Joseph Howe, the fiery 19th-century Nova Scotia nationalist. The quotation, taken from one of Bob's father's schoolbooks, reads:

In every village in our infant country we have the quiet graves of those who subdued the wilderness, who beautified the land by their toil, and left not only the fruits of their labours, but the thoughts and feelings that cheered them in their solitude, to cheer and stimulate us amidst the inferior trials and multiplied enjoyments of a more advanced state of society . . .

That is the way the McMichaels feel about the Collection,

and they believe it will still be here centuries from now to cheer and stimulate a future world and act as a link between the ages.

THE ARTISTS

The group of seven artists whose pictures are here exhibited have for several years held a like vision concerning Art in Canada. They are all imbued with the idea that an Art must grow and flower in the land before the country will be a real home for its people . . . The artists invite adverse criticism. Indifference is the greatest evil they have to contend with . . .

Group of Seven catalogue 1920

Momentous times! A group of young rebels were showing their paintings at the Art Museum of Toronto.

It was a challenge to Canadians to throw off the notion that the only good painting was European painting and the only good techniques were techniques used by painters in other lands.

The foreword continued scornfully

The so-called Art lovers . . . will refuse to recognize anything that does not come up to the commercialized, imported standard of the picture-sale room. They prefer to enrich the salesman than accept the productions by artists native to the land . . .

It was tough talk from tough men. Tender men, yes, but men tough enough to leave the comfort and security of the studio and to backpack into the bush and paint Canada as it really was.

Pugnaciously quoting the Irish writer A.E. Russell, the catalogue laid it on the line:

. . . if a people do not believe they can equal or surpass the stature of any humanity which has been upon this world, then they had better emigrate and become servants to some superior people.

Later, they were to mellow, but in 1920, they were angry young men challenging the critics and the Canadian art establishment, just as their country was throwing off the shackles of colonialism and becoming a nation in its own right. They took their case to the people, and somewhere the two, the painting of the Group and the nationalism of Canada, merged and became one.

It all began in the days leading up to the First World War. Tom Thomson, J.E.H. MacDonald, Arthur Lismer, Frederick Varley, Frank Johnston and Frank Carmichael were working at Grip Limited in Toronto as commercial artists, They met Lawren Harris and later invited A.Y. Jackson, whose work they admired, to come from Montreal and join them.

In 1913, Lawren Harris, in partnership with art patron Dr. James MacCallum, built the Studio Building overlooking Rosedale Ravine in Toronto. Tom Thomson shared a studio in it with Frank Carmichael for a time, but he preferred to live and work in a small wooden building on the property which inevitably became known as Thomson's Shack. Thomson, then in his late thirties, had shown no particular talent until 1912, when in Algonquin Park, he had finally broken through the fetters of traditional technique and begun painting the land in a new way.

Like the future members of the Group, Thomson discovered that the light of Canada and the shapes and forms of its landscape demanded a new approach. The others were encouraged by Thomson to visit the Park and Lismer wrote home from it in 1914: "The country is a revelation to me." It was in the fall, working side by side at Oxtongue River, that Jackson painted his famous *Red Maple* and Thomson painted what is considered a breakthrough panel *Red Leaves*. From that point on, for the remaining three years of his life, Thomson painted Algonquin Park with broad strokes, a joyous freedom and a richness of colour unparalleled in the history of Canadian art. Thoreau MacDonald, the son of J.E.H. MacDonald, wrote of Thomson: "The north woods were in his bones and he brought his sketches out of the bush as naturally as a hunter brings out fish or partridge." His drowning in a canoe accident in the Park in 1917 shocked the others and made them even more determined to paint Canada their way. At war in France, more than 3,000 miles away, A.Y. Jackson wrote to J.E.H. MacDonald:

> *Without Tom the north country seems a desolation of bush and rock, he was the guide, the interpreter, and we the guests partaking of his hospitality so generously given . . . my debt to him is almost that of a new world, the north country, and a truer artist's vision.*

And later, when a cairn was erected at Canoe Lake, where Thomson had drowned, the text by J.E.H. MacDonald for the tablet read:

> *He lived humbly but passionately with the wild. It made him brother to all untamed things of nature. It drew him apart and revealed itself wonderfully to him. It sent him out from the woods only to show these revelations through his art; and it took him to itself at last.*

After the war, the vast Algoma region north of Lake Superior became painting country for the Group. For Harris, MacDonald and Jackson it was the inspiration for some of their greatest achievements. Algoma, in 1918, was a wilderness where virtually no one lived and travelling was very difficult.

It was Harris's inspired idea to rent a boxcar from the Algoma Central Railway and have it shunted onto sidings near choice painting locations. His letter to J. E. H. MacDonald indicates the excitement they felt.

. . . Well James, Me Boy, down on your knees and give great gobs of thanks to Allah! . . . we have a car waiting us on the Algoma Central!!! A car to live in, eat in and work out of. They will move about as we desire and leave us on auspicious sidings that we may proceed to biff the landscape into a cocked hat at our sweet will . . .

Now, young fellah, you can take with you what you will as we settle into our movable home. The next morning after we leave Toronto — easel, books, grand piano, etc. . . . Your only real essentials as I see it now, are blankets (lots of them), warm clothes and sketching outfit. I also suggest a rig that will enable you to keep dry and sketch in the rain.

We leave Toronto the evening of Tues. the 10th or Wed. the 11th of Sept., arrive Soo next day — board our car and stay therein and thereout for three weeks or so, having supplies, mail etc. left us by passing trains every second day or so.

Our palace is a work car, with stove, cooking utensils . . . and four bunks built therein . . .

Tell Frank the "Noos" and warn him re blankets and sufficient paints — warm clothes,

Yours,

Lawren

In September, 1918, Harris, MacDonald, Frank Johnston and Dr. MacCallum made the first boxcar trip. Varley and Jackson were still overseas as Canadian war artists and Lismer was principal of an art college in Halifax. In September, 1919, Harris, MacDonald, Johnston and Jackson made the second trip, this time for a month. During it, Jackson painted the sketch for *First Snow, Algoma,* and MacDonald painted the sketches for *Leaves in the Brook, Algoma Waterfall* and *Forest Wilderness.* The canvases from these sketches are now in the McMichael Collection.

After this trip, the Group decided to hold its first show which probably did more to focus attention on Canadian art than any other previous event. As more Canadians penetrated the country the Group had painted, many of them came to realize that there really were clouds like that, and lakes like that, and rocks like that, and that clouds sometimes did march across a sunset sky, mackerel fashion, just as the Group had painted them. Further exhibitions in 1921, 1922, 1925, 1926, 1930 and 1931 drew increasing understanding and more favourable receptions. After 1920, the Group returned occasionally to Algoma but there was a tendency for its members to travel and paint as individuals further apart.

The original members of the Group were Lawren Harris, A.Y. Jackson, J.E.H. MacDonald, Frederick Varley, Arthur Lismer, Frank Johnston and Frank Carmichael. Johnston resigned in 1922, and A.J. Casson, Edwin Holgate and Lionel Lemoine FitzGerald were added in 1926, 1931, and 1932 respectively.

In 1920, when the Group held its first exhibition, its catalogue bore the stylized logo Group of Seven, and the name stuck. No one ever has been able to pin down who originated the name. Whenever A.Y. Jackson was asked, he always managed to become deliberately vague. The name later was to provide detractors of the Group with considerable merriment, because at times, the Group consisted of six members and once had eight.

To be a member of the Group, you needed two things — a love of painting and a love of the outdoors. There were no helicopters in the early years of this century and few airplanes, and if a man wanted to paint a remote lake, he got to it by canoe. Stiff aching muscles and insect bites came with the territory. But alone or in each other's company, the members of the Group discovered a joy and fraternity that speaks for itself in their paintings. There was never anything musty about them or their work. They were as alive and vibrant as the wilderness itself.

Everyone, however, was not as enthusiastic about the Group's paintings as its members were. When they held their 1920 exhibition, criticism was mixed with some news accounts reporting praise. Traditional European art was accepted as the norm, and the critics and art establishment still felt comfortable with it.

It was not until the British Empire Exhibition at Wembley in 1924 that the Group received almost unanimous praise from British critics. The Trustees of the National Gallery at Ottawa recognized the importance of these favourable reviews and published them in that year ". . . to show the very great interest and high opinion of Canadian art held abroad . . ." But acceptance from patrons was a long time coming. As late as 1958, the McMichaels were able to pick up Group sketches for $150 that now sell for $15,000 and more.

Such were the perils of earning a living as a painter in Canada at the time the Group was formed that only Harris and Jackson were able to work full time at it, and the latter only because he lived so frugally. The others worked as commercial artists, graphic designers and teachers, and Thomson was a part-time guide and forest ranger.

Varley lived in Vancouver and taught at the Vancouver School of Art, and like him, Lismer and Carmichael also taught.

Harris, in Vancouver, was evolving a new style marked by great simplicity and power. MacDonald, though he spent the winters in Toronto as a teacher and later principal of the Ontario College of Art, travelled west every summer from 1924 to 1930.

The threads of communication had thinned, and after MacDonald died in 1932 the Group disbanded to make way for the formation of a more broadly based group called The Canadian Group of Painters. The new group founded in 1933 offered a continuing forum for progressive artists with studios across the breadth of the nation. Members of the Group such as Emily Carr, David Milne, Jock MacDonald and many others, were to broaden the horizons of Canadian art through the next four decades until the enlarged Group disbanded in 1969.

In the mid-twenties, Jackson said prophetically:
I can hear the young painter up north say to his pal, "There's the trail those academic Johnnies, the Group of Seven, blazed."

He was talking not only of the trails they blazed for future painters, but of the frontiers they opened in the hearts of their countrymen through the haunting beauty of their work.

The wealth of Canadian art treasures that forms The McMichael Canadian Collection is due largely to those who have generously given their cherished works of art. They were willing to share these with all Canadians and, in so doing, have placed this wider interest above their own personal pride and pleasure of ownership. Each work of art given to The Collection bears a plaque which identifies the donor and lends recognition to those who have assisted in making The Collection the symbol of national art it has become over the years. The philosophy of having virtually the entire collection on display allows a permanent tribute to both the donor and the artist. They will be held in the highest esteem by this and future generations.

Woodland Waterfall. 1916
123.0 x 132.5

TOM THOMSON 1877-1917

The life of Tom Thomson was the pure stuff of legends. Most of his later years were lived alone in the forest. His early death, in mysterious circumstances, plus the meteor-like briefness of his dazzling career, combined to turn him into a national icon of art.

Tom Thomson's art has always had a special meaning for Bob and Signe McMichael, as it has for most Canadians. The magic of his style, his close identification with the wilderness and his legendary career have put him to the forefront of an art that is truly Canadian. The name of Tom Thomson is synonymous with the search for a native art expression. The magnificent selection from his production in the McMichael Canadian Collection allows one to see his search through its total evolution.

Although he was only forty when he drowned in Algonquin Park's Canoe Lake, Thomson achieved an astonishing body of work. His large canvases are few, but his small oil panels number into hundreds. He managed to produce these while spending much of his time as a guide and forest ranger.

Thomson's finest and most characteristic art was compressed into a brief period of three years, from 1914 until his death in the summer of 1917. Thomson started very slowly as an artist. He was doing dull, imitative, and not very accomplished drawings of figures and landscapes well into his thirties, an age when most artists have already achieved a personal authority of style. In the McMichael Collection examples of these early founderings are available to provide valuable comparisons with the achievements of his last years. It is difficult to believe that these earlier pieces were done only a few years before Thomson first visited Algonquin Park and became, virtually overnight, a totally equipped landscape painter.

In the little *Fairy Lake* sketch of 1910, Thomson gives some inkling of his ability to capture mood, but it is still a painting dictated by the subject: the artist is not in full command. In the canvas *Afternoon, Algonquin Park*, Thomson begins to find his true style—that combination of exact observation and spirited execution that was his own. Then in such 1915 sketches as *Burned Over Land* and *The Log Flume*, he breaks into the radiant colour and commanding brushwork that led to the climactic intensity of his last 1917 studies.

The McMichael Canadian Collection exhibits many of Thomson's most masterly late sketches. It would be difficult to imagine more spirited and compelling landscapes than these small masterpieces. From the pictorial resources of Algonquin Park, Thomson mined such glowing compositions as *Autumn Birches*, *Tea Lake Dam*, *Tamaracks*, *Ragged Pine* and *Autumn Colour*, all painted in 1915 and 1916. These on-the-spot sketches were the work of a few hours at most, but they will survive as long as a love for Canadian art survives.

Born in Claremont, Ontario, in 1877, Tom Thomson spent his boyhood in Leith, near Owen Sound. He wandered briefly to Seattle, Washington, then settled in Toronto as a commercial artist, but finally found his spiritual and creative home in Algonquin Park. Today, in the McMichael Canadian Collection and its natural surroundings, with his shack close by, Tom Thomson has found a different sort of home, where millions in the future will be able to see our land through his eyes.

In tribute to Thomson, it would be difficult to improve on J.E.H. MacDonald's description of him, written for a memorial cairn in Algonquin Park: "He lived humbly but passionately with the wild. It made him brother to all untamed things of nature. It drew him apart and revealed itself wonderfully to him. It sent him out from the woods only to show these revelations through his art. And it took him to itself at last."

Kleinburg Celebrates Canada

With 1,500 works of art and early provincial cooking

by Jeremy Ferguson

T he Ontario village of Kleinburg, with its storybook
storefronts, nearby farms
and rolling green countryside, qualifies as one of the
loveliest in Canada. What makes Kleinburg a marvelous day trip out of Toronto
are two attractions celebrating Cana-
diana—the McMichael Canadian Collection, one of the country's finest art
galleries, and the Doctor's House and
Livery, a restaurant dedicated to old
Ontario cooking.

The **McMichael Canadian Collection**
is really the heart of the place, although
it is doubtful Robert and Signe McMichael foresaw this when they bought
their first Canadian painting, by Lawren
Harris, 25 years ago for their log home
in the wilderness. The McMichaels'
spread is now publicly owned and ad-

carved teller's cage from Quebec. The
quilt over the rocker was made in 1810
by MacEachern's great-great-great-
great grandmother. The beam over the
fireplace—always crackling away in
cool weather—is the main beam from
Doc Robinson's barn.

The same care is given to the food.
Painstaking research sent MacEachern
as far back as an 1841 Canadian cook-
book. "The pioneers simply used what
was fresh," he says. "They'd never
been to Paris or heard of the Cordon
Bleu, but they put fowl and ham and
cheese together, found it tasted good
and called it split fowl and leathery
ham." Freshness is still the keyword. In
spring, MacEachern and his family pick
fiddleheads for the vegetables of the
day; in autumn, they find puffballs for
puffball soup.

Specialties of the Livery menu is

magnificent parkland filled with wildlife, maples, pines and silence. The original log house has mushroomed into a log palace with some 32 galleries containing more than 1,500 works of art.

Deceptively small and rustic on the exterior, it invariably amazes those who drop in for a casual visit and wind up spending the whole day. The visitor is confronted by more than 500 paintings by some of Canada's finest artists. There are works by men such as Lawren Harris, Arthur Lismer and A. Y. Jackson, who captured the Ontario northland as no one else ever has. There are also more than 80 paintings by Tom Thomson, hailed in many quarters as Canada's greatest artist, plus Indian and Eskimo prints, paintings and sculptures—everything set against richly textured surfaces of brick, barn board and burlap.

The collection's West Coast Gallery contains some 3,000 square feet of floor space and houses everything from Indian ceremonial masks to Emily Carr paintings and a Kwakiutl Indian totem pole. The masks, powerful images from a vanished way of life, speak for many tribes—the Kwakiutl, Haida, Bella Coola, Nootka, Tsimshian and others. The totem pole is from a deserted island off the tip of Vancouver Island.

The shack in which Tom Thomson lived and painted was moved from the Toronto suburb of Rosedale to the McMichaels' property. It contains the

MW160/12

last full-size canvases appeared on the market and was added to the collection at a cost of $250,000.

In 1964, the McMichaels, aware that their private passion had burgeoned into a public treasure, donated the works to the Province of Ontario. Ontario agreed to maintain, protect and staff the collection. The McMichaels elected to stay on as curators.

The traffic to the galleries eventually gave birth to the **Doctor's House and Livery** restaurant. By 1961, bulldozer progress threatened the old house, dating back to 1867, in which local doctor Thomas Robinson lived and practiced for 46 years until his death in 1929. A local woman, Torchy MacEachern, bought the charming frame house to save it from being razed. Ten years later, it was obvious Kleinburg needed an eatery, and the Doctor's House opened for light lunches and weekend dinners.

Torchy's son John, a seasoned restaurateur, converted the Doctor's House into a full-time restaurant serving the foods of Ontario's early settlers. The crowds spilled over, and a year later he shifted the restaurant operation to the livery behind the house; the latter was transformed into **The Side Door** gift shop.

From the outset, John MacEachern was determined the room would have character, and how well he succeeded is immediately apparent. In place of a cashier's wicket is an antique, hand-

wine. Ontario pheasant comes tender and moist, slathered in a smoked bacon and cream sauce. Rack of lamb makes you wish for more. Desserts are homemade apple pie with nippy Cheddar cheese and peach-and-sour cream pie.

After the McMichael Canadian Collection and the Livery came a plethora of arts and crafts shops. The latest and most amiable of these is the **Mouse House,** a flamboyant enterprise operated by two Kleinburg women, Susan Grafi and Gail McCormack. For sale herein are all manner of mice. There are country mice, city mice, naked mice, elaborately costumed mice, everything from marzipan mice at 80 cents to crystal mice at $65. It's next door to the Doctor's House, and the Kleinburg visitor, it is presumed, will make the moused of it. ∎

How and Where

From downtown Toronto, follow Queen Elizabeth Way west to Islington Avenue, and drive north about 20 minutes to Kleinburg; or drive north to Highway 401, west to Highway 400, and north to Major Mackenzie Drive into Kleinburg.

The McMichael Canadian Collection is open noon to 5.30 Tuesday through Sunday. Admission is free: 416-893-1121. The Doctor's House and Livery is open noon to 3 for lunch and 5 P.M. to 1 A.M. for dinner, Tuesday through Sunday; 893-1615 for reservations.

ILLUSTRATED BY SUSAN WILLIAM KUF

Travel & Leisure News, age 1989

◀ **Summer Shore, Georgian Bay.** c. 1916
72.5 x 77.5

Afternoon Algonquin Park. 1915
64.2 x 81.7

Sunrise. 1916-17
21.6 x 26.7

Snow Shadows. 1915
21.2 x 26.7

Sombre Day. 1916
21.5 x 26.7

Spring Breakup. 1916
21.6 x 26.7

Autumn, Algonquin Park. 1915
51.8 x 41.9

Pine Cleft Rocks. 1915
21.3 x 27.7

TOM THOMSON

TOM THOMSON

Moonlight and Birches. 1916-17
22.0 x 27.0

Spring Flood. 1915
21.2 x 26.7

Autumn Birches. 1916
21.6 x 26.7

Black Spruce in Autumn. 1916
21.5 x 26.8

TOM THOMSON

Beech Grove. 1915-16
21.7 x 26.5

Windy Day. 1916-17
21.5 x 26.6

New Life After Fire. 1914
21.5 x 26.7

Aura Lee Lake. 1915
21.3 x 26.7

Pine Island. 1914
21.7 x 26.7

The Log Flume. 1915
21.5 x 26.7

Islands, Canoe Lake. 1915
21.2 x 26.7

Backwater. 1915
21.5 x 26.7

Algonquin, October. 1915
21.6 x 26.8

Summer Day. 1915-16
21.6 x 26.8

A.Y. JACKSON 1882-1974

The name of A.Y. Jackson has been more closely associated with the McMichael Canadian Collection than that of any other artist. Jackson encouraged and supported the creation of the Collection from its beginnings and helped formulate its early character. It was ideally fitting that, after a lifetime of travel he chose to spend his last years as an artist-in-residence at the Kleinburg gallery. There, he was available to meet and advise any of the interested public about the Group of Seven and their contemporaries. For thousands of visitors—especially schoolchildren—to the Collection, "A.Y." was a warm link with a heroic creative period of Canada's past.

The artistic Odyssey of A.Y. Jackson began in Montreal, where he studied as a young man under William Brymner, who also taught fellow Group member, Edwin Holgate. After studying and painting in Europe, he was encouraged by Lawren Harris and J.E.H. MacDonald to settle in Toronto in 1913. The next year, he took up residence with other future members of the Group of Seven in the famous Studio Building in Toronto's Rosedale Valley. Jackson remained at the Studio Building for most of his life, using it as a base from which he sojourned in his countless painting trips that covered the breadth of Canada.

Over a career of more than six decades, Jackson came to know the geographic features of this country better than any other man. He came to know it intimately from the vantage point of his sketch box, from Newfoundland to the Pacific and into the farthest recesses of the Arctic. During his wanderings, he did not forget the presence of man at the edge of the wilderness. He affectionately portrayed Quebec's pastel-hued rural villages, Ontario's northern mining towns, ice-bound Eskimo settlements and British Columbia's Indian enclaves.

Jackson's art forms a visual diary proclaiming pictorial paeans to the physical shape of his homeland. From its pages emerge the bleak Arctic tundras, the glories of Algoma autumns, the gently swelling forms of the Prairies, the rolling hills of the Laurentians, the ice-blue features of the Polar icecaps and the thrusting challenge of the Rockies. As an artist, Jackson was of necessity often a loner, but he took an infectious enjoyment in his fellow men. Wherever he went, he made new friends and admirers until, in the end, he became in the minds of most of his countrymen, the living symbol of Canadian art. In a more specific way, Jackson used his enormous energy and experience to teach and lecture between his painting journeys.

The more than 150 works in the McMichael Canadian Collection present an unrivalled survey of A.Y. Jackson's art from its beginnings. Here are to be seen all of the gradual stylistic progressions that marked his career from the delicate watercolour, *Elms and Wildflowers* of 1902, to drawings of Newfoundland executed half a century later. Among his oils done early in this century are the subtle impressionist panel of *Venice*, 1908 and the canvas *Sand Dunes, Etaples* of 1912. From this same formative period, the McMichael Canadian Collection includes some unexpected subjects by Jackson. *The Parlour* of 1910 is an interior study of Jackson's aunt's home in Berlin, Ontario, now Kitchener. In the background of this painting may be seen the Dutch masterpiece, *Incredulity of St. Thomas*, by the seventeenth-century artist, Hendrick Terbrugghen, which now hangs in the Rijksmuseum in Amsterdam. Two other unusual early compositions are a still life of *Dahlias* and *Figure Against the Sky*, both painted in 1913. From that period on, with the exception of the witty self-portrait *Père Raquette*, Jackson appears in the collection as the great painter of the Canadian landscape so familiar to every Canadian.

Barns. 1926
21.6 x 26.7

Sunlit Tapestry. 1939
71.5 x 91.6

Winter Morning, St. Tite des Caps. 1934
54.1 x 67.0

Fishing Village, Gaspe Shore. 1934
26.7 x 34.2

Quebec Village. c. 1930
21.4 x 26.7

Eskimos and Tent. 1927
21.5 x 26.8

Grey Day, Laurentians. 1933
54.0 x 66.2

Indian Home. 1926
21.1 x 26.6

Skeena Crossing. 1926
54.0 x 66.8

Père Raquette. 1921
80.0 x 64.8

The Red Maple. 1914
21.7 x 26.9

A. Y. JACKSON

Iceberg at Godhaven. 1930
21.1 x 26.7

Lake in the Hills. 1922
65.0 x 82.8

Nellie Lake. 1933
76.9 x 81.4

A. Y. JACKSON

Sand Dunes, Etaples, France. 1912
54.6 x 64.8

Cathedral at Ypres. 1917
21.7 x 26.8

Venice. 1911
21.3 x 26.2

October, Lake Superior. 1923
21.2 x 26.6

Above Lake Superior. 1924
116.8 x 147.3

Superstition Island, Great Bear Lake. 1950
53.3 x 66.0

The Parlour. 1910
36.0 x 41.1

River, St. Urbain. 1935
21.2 x 26.8

Alberta Foothills. 1937
64.0 x 81.2

Church at St. Urbain, 1931
54.0 x 66.6

J.E.H. MACDONALD 1873-1932

No Canadian landscape painter possessed a richer command of colour and pigment than J.E.H. MacDonald. His finest achievements weave together glowing pigment, brushwork and design into tapestry-like compositions. The best of these are now familiar touchstones of Canadian culture.

MacDonald was known to his fellow-artists as a gentle, reserved man, yet his paintings are among the most powerful by the Group of Seven and present the most commanding orchestrations of colour. MacDonald could merge surprising combinations of oranges, reds, greens and violets together with dramatic and controlled effect. His early skills as a draughtsman enabled him to join brilliant drawing to his singular colour sense. His actual brushwork is at once disciplined and vigorous. His best on-the-spot sketches possess an intensity and freshness of execution not dissimilar from Van Gogh.

MacDonald began his career as a commercial designer and in that capacity met Tom Thomson and encouraged the younger artist to paint landscapes. MacDonald was undoubtedly the biggest single influence upon Thomson. From his earliest years, MacDonald was a natural teacher, eager to share his knowledge, enthusiasm and experience. Many painters benefited from his instruction and the last ten years of his life were devoted to teaching at the Ontario College of Art. He was principal of the College when he died in 1932.

In 1909, MacDonald was one of the first to paint in Northern Ontario. His early impressions of that period are muted, almost monochrome studies. In the following years, he was laying the disciplined groundwork for such blazing outbursts of colour as *The Tangled Garden* of 1916, a *tour de force* of hue and texture that represented a revolution in Canadian painting. MacDonald usually reserved his rebel statements to paint itself, a medium which he knew could speak more eloquently for him than words. When MacDonald did write for publication, it was usually lyric poetry and a number of these were collected together in the volume *West By East*, illustrated by his son, Thoreau.

MacDonald travelled less frequently than many other members of the Group of Seven. His obligations as a commercial artist and later as a teacher limited his sketching journeys. Of all the places he did visit, the Algoma area of Northern Ontario inspired him the most. What Mont Ste. Victoire was to Cezanne or Arles to Van Gogh, Algoma was to MacDonald. It represented for him a landscape talisman that brought forth his most complete creative response. In Algoma, his art reached its zenith. In brief trips to the area in 1918 and 1919, he amassed the brilliant sketches from which he composed such unforgettable masterpieces as *The Solemn Land, Leaves In The Brook, Autumn In Algoma, Falls On The Montreal River, Algoma Waterfall* and *Forest Wilderness*.

In the McMichael Canadian Collection, MacDonald is represented by several famous canvases and an unrivalled selection of his oil sketches, on panel. Among his major works on view is the great close-up composition, *Leaves In The Brook* and the magnificent, panoramic *Forest Wilderness*, originally in the R.S. McLaughlin Collection. These two works are rivalled in textural and chromatic richness by *Algoma Waterfall*, painted at the same period. The later, more restrained, mountain phase of MacDonald's art is well represented by *Goat Range, Rocky Mountains*, of 1932. MacDonald's small, on-the-spot sketches rival Thomson's in their variety, richness of colour and technical dexterity. Each one of these marvelous small creations is a complete painting in itself. Although many did serve as models for later studio canvases, MacDonald clearly considered his sketches totally realized impressions at the time of their execution.

Buckwheat Field. 1923
21.3 x 26.4

Lodge Interior, Lake O'Hara. 1925
21.4 x 26.6

Artist's Home and Orchard. 1927
21.5 x 26.3

J. E. H. MacDONALD

Silver Swamp, Algoma. 1919
21.4 x 26.6

Northern Lights. 1916
20.2 x 25.4

Aurora, Georgian Bay. 1931
21.5 x 26.7

Forest Wilderness. 1921
121.9 x 152.4

J. E. H. MacDONALD

Autumn, Algoma. 1920
21.4 x 26.7

Beaver Dam and Birches. 1919
21.5 x 26.5

Wild Ducks. 1916
20.2 x 25.4

Lichen Covered Shale Slabs. 1930
21.4 x 26.6

Agawa Canyon. 1920
21.3 x 26.6

Mountain Stream. 1930
21.4 x 26.6

Moose Lake, Algoma. 1919
21.3 x 26.5

Cathedral Peak, Lake O'Hara. 1927
21.4 x 26.6

LAWREN HARRIS

1885-1970

Lawren Harris was the prime leader of Canadian art for many decades. He was the main force that brought together and joined the varying talents and temperaments which formed the Group of Seven. For many years after the disbanding of the Seven, he remained a powerful force in Canadian painting, aiding and encouraging Emily Carr and a host of younger artists. He was also a founder of the now famous Canadian Group of Painters, which succeeded the Group of Seven in 1933.

Harris was a constant experimenter. He did not hesitate to launch into a new style when he was convinced that he had completely explored the one preceding. No painter of his country approached the variety of pictorial expression commanded by Harris. Throughout a long lifetime of searching, his work passed through five major periods—ranging from the impressionistic Toronto "house" paintings of the early 1900's, through richly pigmented, tapestry-like landscapes of Algoma, dramatically designed compositions of the North Shore of Lake Superior, the blue and white crystal-like compositions of the Arctic and the Rockies, to his last phase of total abstraction.

Born in Brantford, Ontario, in 1885, Harris' career took him to Toronto, Massachusetts, New Mexico and Vancouver; but wherever he went Harris held firm to his dedication to the native Canadian outlook he first stated in the catalogue of the 1920 Group of Seven exhibition: "The group of seven artists whose pictures are here exhibited have for several years held a like vision concerning art in Canada. They are all imbued with the idea that an art must grow and flower in the land before the country will be a real home for its people."

Harris' paintings have indeed helped make Canada a real spiritual home for millions of its people. His vision was primed for the far horizons of his own country, and he had need to nurture his eyes on its open spaces. He made several trips to Europe, but each time he returned home complaining that "everything was too close." He recognized the supreme traditions of European art, but his own pressing desire was to create something individual and fresh. In his finest works he achieved that goal magnificently.

It would be difficult to visualize a richer representation of Lawren Harris' varied styles than can be seen in the McMichael Canadian Collection. His career began with a series of almost sombre landscapes painted in 1910 and 1911, mostly of the environs of Toronto. These undistinguished early efforts were followed by works done on trips to the Laurentians, Algonquin Park and Georgian Bay in 1912, when he emerged as a painter with a developing style of his own. The resonant gold and brown Laurentian studies is typified in the Collection by *Laurentians* 1912. From the same year come his *Algonquin Park Sunburst* and *Old Houses Toronto*. In the years between 1912 and 1920, Harris portrayed his houses and landscapes in heavy tapestry-like paint textures. Among the brilliant sketches from this period on view are *Algoma Woodland* 1919, *Beaver Dam* 1919, *Montreal River* 1920 and *Red Maples* 1920.

Of Harris' monumental blue and white phase which began in the early 1920's, the Collection owns many masterpieces, including *Pic Island* 1923, *Lake Superior Island* 1923, *Mt. Lefroy* 1930, *Mountains and Lake* 1929 and *Lake and Mountains* 1927. The superb Arctic paintings of 1930 include *Eclipse Sound and Bylot Island*, *Ellesmere Island* and the monumental *Icebergs, Davis Strait*. These Arctic works of 1930-31 seem an inevitable extension of his Lake Superior and Rocky Mountain experiences. From unpopulated lands of rock he moved into a scene even more remote where there was almost no land, only floating ice and sky and water.

The Arctic voyage and the pictures resulting from it virtually brought Harris' career as a landscape painter to a close and ushered in his period of non-objective art.

Northern Lake. c. 1923
82.7 x 103.0

Snow, Rocky Mountains. 1925
26.8 x 35.3

Country North of Lake Superior. 1921
26.0 x 35.0

Algoma Canyon. 1923
30.1 x 37.8

The Ice House. 1923
30.0 x 38.1

Shimmering Water, Algonquin Park. 1922
82.3 x 101.8

Lake Superior Cliffs. 1921
30.2 x 38.0

Newfoundland Coast. 1921
26.8 x 34.9

LAWREN HARRIS

Eclipse Sound and Bylot Island. 1930
30.2 x 38.0

Algoma Reflections. 1919
26.4 x 35.1

Montreal River. 1920
26.9 x 34.8

South End of Maligne Lake. 1925
27.0 x 35.2

Lake and Mountains. 1927
30.3 x 38.0

Little House. 1911
19.9 x 14.2

Lake Superior Island. 1923
74.2 x 89.0

Mount Temple. 1924
30.5 x 38.1

ARTHUR LISMER 1885-1969

Arthur Lismer was the great teacher of the Group of Seven. From 1915 until his death, he taught at many institutions, including the Ontario College of Art, the Nova Scotia College of Art, the Montreal Museum of Fine Arts and McGill University. He devoted much of his life to directing art education for children and received wide international recognition for his achievements in the field. After founding children's classes at the Art Gallery of Toronto in 1929, he was invited to South Africa and Columbia University to initiate courses in the field of art education.

As a teacher and painter, Lismer remained eternally youthful. He possessed an infectious wit and humour which expressed themselves in both words and images. As the Group of Seven's pictorial Boswell, Lismer created a brilliant series of caricatures portraying his colleagues during their meetings and sketching trips. Many of these rapid, visual commentaries round out the outstanding collection of Lismer's works in the McMichael Collection.

Lismer achieved the richest landscape drawings of the Group. These were usually done as ends in themselves and not as studies for paintings. Most of these black and white landscape studies are executed in brush or reed pen and are almost lush in their impact. The best of Lismer's drawings are at the very pinnacle of Canadian graphic art. Marked by a confident

bravura, their spirited calligraphy recalls the sweeping shorthand of the finest Oriental masters.

Lismer painted in many parts of Canada. The extent of his travels is well represented in the McMichael Canadian Collection. His fondness for the Maritimes is reflected in works done as far apart in time as *Maritime Village* of 1919 and *Red Anchor*, painted thirty-five years later. The Lake Superior area of Northern Ontario, Quebec and British Columbia are also represented in his sketches and canvases.

Like F.H. Varley, Arthur Lismer attended the Sheffield School of Art in that English city where he was born, and later spent a period at the Antwerp Academy in Belgium. Thus, when he emigrated to Canada in 1911, he was a completely trained artist in an academic tradition. It was the impact of the Canadian landscape, especially that of Northern Ontario, that released Lismer's vigorous sense of design and colour to their utmost. As early as 1914, he was expressing his enthusiasm for the wilderness of Algonquin Park in both paint and words. On his very first trip to the Park, he wrote: "The first night spent in the north and the thrilling days after were turning points in my life". Such letters reveal the eagerness and eloquence he was later to utilize as a spokesman in defence of his own work and that of his fellow members of the Group of Seven.

Although Lismer painted in many parts of Canada, he is best known as the Group of Seven's painter-biographer of the Georgian Bay district. His lush oil sketches of the Bay's vegetation and pine-etched island horizons compose the richest part of his life's work. Summer after summer, he returned to Georgian Bay to search out the lichen-made patterns of its rocks and to track with brush and pen the tangle of its undergrowth. The canvas *Canadian Jungle* in the McMichael Canadian Collection is a key example of Lismer's consuming interest in texture in nature. *Evening Silhouette* is his vision of the Bay islands at their most romantic. The radiant and compelling *Bright Land* captures the essence of Lismer, brilliant, happy, and eternal optimist who justified his joyful faith in life through his long, outgiving career.

Rain in the North Country. 1920
22.2 x 30.8

Dead Tree, Georgian Bay. 1926
32.7 x 40.6

Canadian Jungle. c. 1946
45.8 x 54.6

ARTHUR LISMER

Pine Wrack. 1939
54.6 x 76.2

Stormy Sky, Georgian Bay. 1922
30.3 x 40.4

Lake Superior. 1927
32.3 x 40.1

Forest Algoma. 1922
71.1 x 91.4

In My Studio. 1924
90.8 x 76.2

Gusty Day, Georgian Bay. 1920
22.8 x 30.3

October on the North Shore. 1927
32.3 x 40.8

Near Amanda, Georgian Bay. 1947
30.2 x 40.4

McGregor Bay. 1933
30.0 x 40.6

Negro Head. 1940
40.2 x 30.6

FREDERICK VARLEY 1881-1969

Varley was the romantic of the Group. His life possessed the same will-of-the-wisp quality that marks many of his poetic landscapes. Until his last years, he was constantly on the move, a questing gypsy of the arts, always, it seems, in search of the perfect landscape, the ideal model.

Varley was tied more closely to European tradition than the other members of the Group. He loved Turner and such other early English landscape painters as Cotnam and Samuel Palmer. His portraits are based in the best tradition of British portrait painting and they have been compared with the works of such masters as Augustus John and Ambrose McEvoy.

In his attitude to his subjects, Varley possessed much of the attitude of a mystic. He usually shunned the hard, clear afternoon light favoured so often by his fellow Group painters. He favoured dawn, dusk and twilight and painted more nocturnes than any of his colleagues. Many of his finest canvases, such as Night Ferry, Vancouver and Moonlight at Lynn are night-pieces. He valued colours for their mystical qualities. Blue, gold, violet and green, he said, were the spiritual hues and these are often dominant in his pictures, even his portraits.

Varley is unquestionably the finest portrayer of people Canada has so far known. He had the imaginative vision, the independence and the technical skills demanded of a great portrait painter. His spirit of independence permitted him to select his sitters and refuse commissions that did not appeal to him.

Varley's best portraits of men are penetrating and vigorous, but unquestionably his most memorable studies are those of women. From time to time throughout his life, Varley would have a special model from whom he realized a series of haunting souvenirs in paint. The best of these combine an affectionate tribute to a favoured sitter with consummate craftsmanship.

Varley's greatest strength as a portrait painter was his masterly draughtsmanship. His drawings in pencil, chalk and ink compose an unrivalled Canadian gallery of graphic art. He could draw with a silver-point sensitiveness without sacrificing any of his characteristic vigor. Varley was a singularly masculine painter and even in his most poetic portraits and atmospheric landscapes, he retains the underlying power of a true master of his craft.

Varley emigrated to Toronto from England in 1912. He was introduced to Algonquin Park by Tom Thomson in 1914 and first came to know the Georgian Bay through Thomson's patron, Dr. J.M. MacCallum. It was in the Bay area that Varley discovered the material for his early Group landscapes, including his masterpiece, *Stormy Weather, Georgian Bay*. A sketch bearing the same title, painted about the same time, is in the McMichael Canadian Collection. The landscape in this sketch is incorporated in the background of the powerful composition, *Indians Crossing Georgian Bay*, also in the Collection. After Georgian Bay, Varley gave his deepest creative loyalty to the British Columbia landscape. There he found an outlet for his romantic nature in a land of mountains, mists and glaciers that would have enchanted Turner. On the Pacific Coast, between 1926 and 1934, Varley painted the most poetic landscapes in Canadian art. These included the lyrical blue and green *Moonlight At Lynn* of 1933 and the expressionistic canvas *Sphinx Glacier, Mt. Garibaldi*, both in the McMichael Canadian Collection. Varley is also well represented in the Collection as a portrait painter and draughtsman. His examples in this genre include one of his finest feminine studies, *Girl In Red* of 1926, the strongly rendered *Negro Head* of 1940 and the eloquent drawings, *Little Girl* of 1923 and *Indian Girl* of 1927.

Dead Tree, Garibaldi Park. c. 1928
30.4 x 38.0

Girl in Red. 1926
53.5 x 52.0

F. H. VARLEY

F. H. VARLEY

Portrait of a Man. 1950
69.5 x 45.6

Little Girl. 1923
36.7 x 28.7

FRANKLIN CARMICHAEL 1890-1945

Many of Franklin Carmichael's finest sketches and canvases were painted near his hometown of Orillia during the early 1920's. During those early Group of Seven years, Carmichael was working fulltime as a commercial designer, and was obliged to find his subject matter on journeys relatively close to Toronto. Despite this, his Orillia paintings lack none of the richness or grandeur of his colleagues' compositions created in the wilderness much further north. Carmichael's early Group period works reveal a rich paint impasto and glowing colour, suggesting an almost buoyant enthusiasm. He delighted in the rich fabric of autumn foliage and excelled in its depiction. Such sketches as *Autumn Tapestry*, *Autumn Woods*, *Scarlet Hilltop* and *Autumn Orillia* in the McMichael Canadian Collection show the artist's love of natural pattern at its best.

Like his younger colleague, A.J. Casson, Carmichael had a fondness for portraying the characteristic stores, barns and houses of rural Ontario settlements. During the 1930's, throughout the southern part of the Province and along the shore of Lake Superior, he found isolated dwellings or small villages from which he composed many watercolours, drawings and a few oils.

His renderings of farmhouses, barns and old homesteads in Whitefish Village, Severn Bridge and many other Ontario communities suggest the same lived-in intimacy as A.Y. Jackson's portrayals of such Quebec villages as St. Tite Des Caps, St. Urbain and St. Pierre.

Franklin Carmichael's large canvases are relative rarities. Although he was dedicated to painting landscape, economic necessity led him to spend much of his lifetime at commercial art and teaching. Unable to concentrate for long periods on major works, he turned to the medium of watercolour for many of his best achievements. His large watercolours possess a crystaline clarity of colour and authority of design in their transparent washes. Carmichael's dedication to watercolour made him a co-founder of the Canadian Society of Painters in Water Colour.

Carmichael's first visit to Lake Superior in 1925 opened up new worlds of form and space to him. The vast panoramas of hills and lakes unrolling before his vision as far as the eye could see captured his imagination. His landscape compositions opened up to include large expanses of sky and simplified silhouettes of whale-back rises, the very opposite to his earlier close-up bush-land paintings. His colour changed also, from thick golds, vermilion, and emerald greens to smoother, dark ultramarines, greys, ochres, siennas and blacks. The emphasis in these compositions became mainly horizontal — a tendency that continued throughout the balance of his career, persisting into the superb impressions of the LaCloche hills painted during the 'thirties. Carmichael's fondness for panoramic compositions can be studied in the McMichael Canadian Collection through such a typical canvas as *Northen Tundra* of 1931, *Grace Lake* of 1933, and such later sketches as *LaCloche Panorama* and *La Cloche Silhouette*, both painted in 1939.

Carmichael was a superb designer and graphic artist. With Edwin Holgate, Carmichael was the only Group of Seven member to devote much attention to the art of wood-engraving. His disciplined dedication to the craft resulted in many sparkling prints, including the pristine small illustrations for the book, *Thorn Apple Tree*, published in 1943. These tiny engravings, which measure less than three by four inches, are replete with vigorously rendered detail and are masterpieces of their kind. They rank Carmichael among the few distinguished book illustrators produced in Canada. Another, very different example of Carmichael's remarkable sense of design can be seen in his crisp tempera translation of landscape, *Waterfall*, in the McMichael Canadian Collection.

Scarlett Hilltop. 1922
24.6 x 30.2

Bolton Hills. c. 1922
24.6 x 30.2

Mirror Lake. 1929
44.6 x 54.3 (sight)

FRANKLIN CARMICHAEL

October Gold. 1922
120.0 x 98.7

FRANKLIN CARMICHAEL

La Cloche Panorama. 1939
25.4 x 30.5

La Cloche Silhouette. 1939
25.5 x 30.5

Spring Garland. c. 1928
25.4 x 30.2

A.J. CASSON 1898-

For the most part, A.J. Casson left the more elemental and epic landscape of the northland to other members of the Group of Seven. His serene pictorial compositions have emerged mainly from southern and central Ontario settings. Particularly, he has been the pictorial biographer of the small communities of Ontario. He has celebrated such towns and villages as Bancroft, Glen Williams, Kleinburg, Parry Sound, Norval and Salem. His crisp, deliberate style has been ideally suited to depict the tidy rustic architecture, with its neat verandahs, almost puritan air of no nonsense form, dressed up with an occasional flight of fancy in the guise of gingerbread "fretwork". Although human figures usually play only bit parts in Casson's canvases, his village paintings are nevertheless redolent of humanity. His houses, barns and churches usually have the air of being lived in. This impression is only fortified when he introduces inhabitants hanging out washing, hauling water or bending before a March blizzard.

Casson was basically a conservative within the Group of Seven. He inherited from his older colleague, Franklin Carmichael, a high regard for craftsmanship. There are no accidents or meaningless flourishes in his creative vocabulaire. Although his small on-the-spot oil panels are executed with a fresh and direct vigor, his larger canvases based on them are composed slowly and with great care. As a result, Casson's stylistic evolution has been a gradual one, moving with a seeming inevitability, and without any sudden leaps into new techniques or thematic novelties.

Casson's independence and respect for tradition brought him the respect of a wide spectrum of artists and allowed him to be a President of the Royal Canadian Academy as well as a member of the pathfinding Group of Seven and the Canadian Group of Painters.

For many years, Casson joined his career as a painter with that of a designer and executive for Sampson-Matthews Limited, a Toronto printing house, where Carmichael and other distinguished Canadian painters were employed. There, Casson produced some of the most outstanding commercial art ever produced in Canada.

Casson is one of the finest watercolourists in Canadian art. He learned his technique from Carmichael and, with him, was a founding member of the Canadian Society of Painters in Water Colour. It is in his watercolours that Casson's design sense can be seen at its purest. Crisp, almost dry, in their rendering, their washes are placed with precision within a careful framework of drawing. Some of Casson's best-known large paintings, such as *The White Pine* in the McMichael Canadian Collection, existed originally as watercolours.

Casson is represented in the McMichael Canadian Collection by half-a-century of his art. The earliest examples are a number of nude studies in pencil and wash executed in 1917. The landscapes on view begin with a number of superb sketches from the early 1920's—*Trees* 1920, *Rock And Sky* 1921, *Haliburton Woods* 1924 and *Poplars* 1925. Casson's most personal vision is first revealed in the *Sombreland*, *Lake Superior* and *Pike Lake* sketches of 1929 and the early village studies, *Norval* and *Kleinburg* of 1929. Casson had by then found his own manner and themes and from then on, through to his LaCloche, Bancroft and Quebec paintings, his evolution was a continuing enrichment of familiar themes.

Kleinburg. c. 1929
23.9 x 28.5

Casson Lake. 1976
30.5 x 38.1

Pike Lake. 1929
42.2 x 50.7 (sight)

Summer Hillside, Kamaniskeg. 1945
50.8 x 60.9

Drowned Land, Algoma. 1918
44.5 x 53.5 (sight)

FRANK JOHNSTON

1888-1949

Frank Johnston's 1918 paintings of Algoma are as compelling as anything done by the Group of Seven at that time. Although he remained with the Group only briefly, Johnston's short contribution to it was a very eloquent one. The best of his sketches of the period are consummately designed, richly painted tangles of branches, evergreens and foliage. From the beginning of his career, Johnston had a highly developed dramatic sense in his approach to nature. In his tempera paintings done shortly after World War I, he captured the immensity of the northern solitudes in compositions bearing such titles as *The Guardian of the Gorge*. Pictorial drama is present, too, in such large northern canvases as *Fire Swept Algoma* of 1920. Like so many of his colleagues, Johnston for many years made his main living as a teacher. After leaving the Group, he turned to teaching for twenty years, first as Principal of the Winnipeg School of Art and then as a teacher at the Ontario College of Art and later as Director of his own Art School on the shores of Georgian Bay. In the latter part of his career, Johnston devoted himself to a technique of almost photographic realism with which he recorded life in Southern Ontario farm and bushland, and life in the Canadian Arctic. These later paintings are executed in a medium which allowed the artist to capture the glitter of sunlight and the smallest details of texture. His obvious technical brilliance made Johnston one of the most popular and financially successful artists of his time.

Moose Pond. 1918
26.4 x 33.8

Patterned Hillside. 1918
26.7 x 33.6

FRANK H. JOHNSTON

Prairie. 1921
18.2 x 22.1

LEMOINE FITZGERALD 1890-1956

LeMoine FitzGerald was the only western Canadian painter to become a member of the Group of Seven. FitzGerald's membership came at the very end of the Group's existence, too late to have any but an honorary significance. He was, in fact, too removed physically, in Winnipeg, and too different in his approach to landscape painting to have fitted in with the Group in their heyday.

FitzGerald was exceedingly individualistic, both as a personality and artist. Although he was involved in teaching at the Winnipeg School of Art for a quarter of a century, he was very much of a loner as a creative painter. His serene, pointilist canvases were achieved mostly during his holidays, using an immensely painstaking technique. It is not surprising that FitzGerald's paintings are few in number when one realizes how slowly his style obliged him to work and how little free creative time was at his disposal.

The paintings FitzGerald did achieve earned him a major place in Canadian art. He might fairly be described as the Seurat or Vermeer of our country's painting. He usually chose the simplest, most commonplace of themes—a garage, a backyard, a few apples, a milk pitcher or a plant in a window—and by the sheer intensity of his vision and refinement of craftsmanship converted these into works of art that, once seen, impress themselves upon the memory. FitzGerald studied for a short period at New York's Art Students League and, as a realist, shared the special magic to intensify ordinary visual experience that marks such great Americans as Charles Sheeler and Georgia O'Keefe.

Because of the limited creative time at his disposal, FitzGerald spent much of it executing drawings in pencil and pen and ink. These are as considered and complete as any of his paintings, and take an outstanding place in Canadian graphic art. They are drawings complete as an end in themselves and not preparatory notes for later development into canvases. In his last years, FitzGerald did a number of pure abstractions which reveal the same stylistic and technical concentration which typify his earlier still-lifes and landscapes. These abstractions represented a logical extension of the artist's lifetime pursuit of form.

The Little Plant. 1947
60.9 x 46.4

LIONEL LEMOINE FITZGERALD

Oak Bluff. 1950
26.7 x 37.4 (sight)

The Embrace. c. 1925
28.0 x 33.8

Tree Trunk. 1939
28.3 x 37.1 (sight)

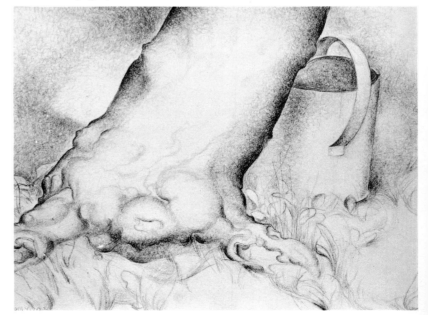

114

The Harvester. 1921
69.0 x 62.2

LIONEL LEMOINE FITZGERALD

DAVID MILNE 1882-1953

David Milne was the quiet man of his generation of Canadian artists. Eloquent in paint, a descriptive writer in his occasional prose, Milne talked little about his art. Unlike the sociable Group of Seven members, Milne only rarely came into contact with his fellow painters. A loner—virtually a recluse—for most of his life, he was the opposite of a self-propagandist. Like Tom Thomson, he allowed his work to speak for him, and it did, in an original, intense and unforgettable way.

As an artist, David Milne made great demands upon his talent. He was a perfectionist, who could paint a dozen variations of the same theme until he was finally satisfied that he had refined his statement down to its essentials. As a result of this approach to art, Milne's compositions may appear deceptively simple at first glance. The depth of experience, judgment and technical skill required to compress such pictorial poetry into a few lines and colours can only be appreciated through acquaintance with his art. Economy of style in Milne's case is the result of an almost monastic dedication. Milne's art is the closest to the great Oriental painters in its eloquent simplicity and pure visual poetry.

The refinement of Milne's style grew through a progression of styles over a period of more than forty years. His canvases before the First World War were heavily pigmented, and boldly drawn in pure vermilions, olive greens, blues, ochres and black.

These brought him international notice in the famous Armory Show at New York in 1913. Milne was one of the many leading Canadian painters who studied at New York's Art Students League and much of his career was spent in the northern part of New York State until 1928. His lean, luminous dry brush watercolours and oils done in the Catskills, the lower Berkshires and the Adirondacks remain among his most commanding achievements. Upon his return to Canada, Milne painted for varying periods, at Timagami, Palgrave, Six Mile Lake and in Toronto. His colour drypoint etchings of Toronto buildings take a special place in his graphic work.

The McMichael Canadian Collection includes significant examples of Milne's achievement from early canvases of the 1914 period to the almost calligraphic watercolours of his last years.

Milne's early New York oils are the most richly coloured and robust of all his works. They are painted with a loaded brush and are almost encrusted in texture. The importance of these early canvases is underlined by the fact that several of them were included in the great, revolutionary Armory Show of 1913 in Manhattan. In that historic exhibition, Milne's work was displayed on the same walls as Picasso, Cezanne, Kandinsky, Matisse and Gauguin. His work can be compared with that of the American master, Maurice Prendergast. In the McMichael Canadian Collection, the early phase of Milne may be seen in the oils *West Saugerties* 1914, *Patsy* 1914, *The Lilies* 1915 and the watercolour *Relaxation* of 1914. In the years following, Milne's style became increasingly leaner in technique and more restricted in colour.

The canvases and watercolours of Boston Corners, Lake Placid and the Adirondacks painted between 1920 and 1928 are lean in execution to the point of a drybrush technique. They are almost Oriental in their subtlety of drawing and restricted hues. In the McMichael Canadian Collection, this phase of Milne's art is richly revealed in such oils as *Boston Corners* 1916, *The Gully* 1920, *Blue Church* 1920, *Haystack* 1923, *Mountains And Clouds* 1925 and the two small canvases of *Clarke's House* of 1923.

Clark's House. 1923
30.5 x 40.6

Clark's House. 1923
30.8 x 40.8

Boston Corners. 1916
45.5 x 52.7

Blue Church. 1920
46.8 x 56.7

Patsy. 1914
51.7 x 61.7

Railway Station. c. 1929
30.9 x 41.0

Pansies and Basket. c. 1947
36.9 x 54.1

Boat Houses in Winter. 1926
41.7 x 51.7

Deer and Decanter. 1939
35.0 x 48.3 (sight)

DAVID B. MILNE

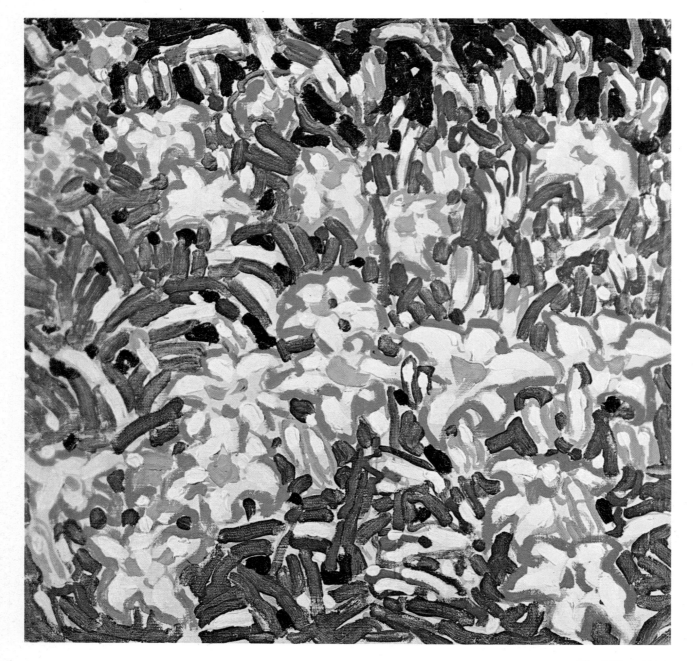

The Lilies. 1914
50.7 x 50.7

Fishermen's Houses, c. 1933
51.0 x 61.2

EDWIN HOLGATE

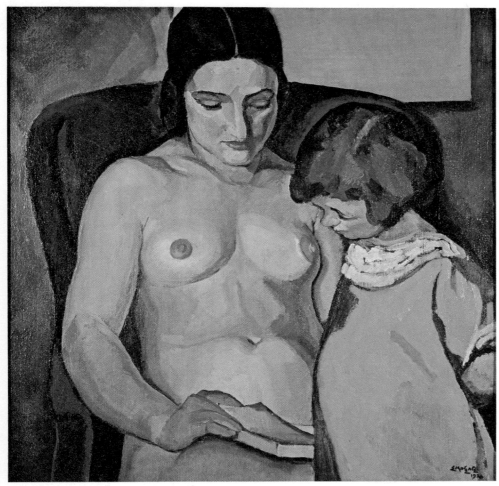

Mother and Daughter. 1926
61.4 x 60.1

EDWIN HOLGATE

1892-1977

Edwin Holgate became a late addition to the Group of Seven in 1931. By then, he had already established a firm reputation for his figure paintings and West Coast and Laurentian landscapes. A student in Montreal under the same William Brymner who had taught A. Y. Jackson, Clarence Gagnon and many other important painters, Holgate early showed a preference for painting humanity, an inclination shared in the Group of Seven only by F. H. Varley. Holgate spent a number of years in Paris painting the figure before returning to Canada in the early 1920's to begin the series of nudes in northern landscapes for which he is best known. Apart from a trip to the Skeena River area of British Columbia with A. Y. Jackson in 1926, Holgate remained a Quebec-based painter. His landscapes were mostly painted in the Laurentians, where he lived much of his life. These are carefully patterned, ruggedly executed compositions, but rarely achieve the creative involvement found in his best figure and portrait studies.

Holgate's robust portraits form an eloquent gallery of Canadians, including lumberjacks, habitants, pilots, and such familiar creative figures as humorist Stephen Leacock. At their finest, there is a masculine monumentality to Holgate's portrayals. He always used a direct, no-nonsense manner of painting which has its origins in the Cezanne oriented painters of the first two decades of the century. The same vigorous approach marks his large portrait drawings in charcoal.

During periods of his career, Holgate shared the same financial difficulties that beset some other members of the Group of Seven. They solved their economic difficulties by teaching,

Melting Snow. 1948
21.6 x 27.0

but Holgate turned to wall decoration. He did many murals of varying distinction, the best known being his effective designs for the Totem Pole Room at Ottawa's Chateau Laurier which regrettably no longer exist except in photographs.

It was only after the Group of Seven years that Holgate finally undertook to teach at the Art Association of Montreal from 1935 to 1940. Many of Canada's most gifted contemporary painters, including Jean-Paul Lemieux and Stanley Cosgrove, benefited from his instruction. Among the talents Holgate brought to his teaching post were his skills as a book illustrator and wood engraver. His wood engravings of nudes and French Canadian interiors include some of the finest of all original Canadian prints. Holgate shared a passionate concern for rural Quebec with such artists as Clarence Gagnon and Horatio Walker. In his own dramatically designed black and white compositions, he made permanent that passing phase of history.

The Cellist. 1923
129.5 x 97.8

Nude. 1922
29.2 x 25.4

CLARENCE GAGNON 1881-1942

Clarence Gagnon was the pictorial bard of rural Quebec. The life and land of the habitant inspired him to some of the most engaging paintings ever made of the Canadian scene. His consummately drawn, high-keyed canvases are vibrant with the atmosphere and activity of French Canada.

Gagnon studied under William Brymner in Montreal and did his earliest records of Quebec at the turn of the century. After five years of study in Paris he returned to Canada in 1919 to begin his pictorial salutes to the colourful settlements of the St. Lawrence and the Laurentians. Although he spent most of his later years in France and Norway, his affections and art remained steeped in the life of his native land.

It was while living in Europe that Gagnon created what must be considered his most ambitious and remarkable creative achievement—the illustrations for the Quebec masterpiece *Maria Chapdelaine* by Louis Hémon. In the fifty-four paintings done to ornament this volume published in Paris in 1934, Gagnon equalled the eloquence of Hémon's symbolic tribute to French Canada with miniature masterpieces of his own.

Nowhere in Canadian annals has illustration reached to such heights as art. And no other Canadian artist possessed the combination of special talents to equal Gagnon's graphic eloquence. The illustrations for *Maria Chapdelaine* combine all of the factual specifics demanded of literary illustration along with

tonal poetry and power of design as paintings in their own right. Sometimes as small as 3 x 3 inches and never averaging more than 10 x 9 inches, these amazing little paintings take a special place in the art of their time. They are, in turn, stark, tragic, gay, brave and tender. They move the emotions as much as they command admiration as art. Their subject matter is as timeless as their expression. From first communion to last rites, here are the vanishing traditions of rural Quebec in their totality.

For the first time, the Maria Chapdelaine illustrations can now be seen and enjoyed at will by the public.

During his lifetime, they were the most treasured possessions of the late Colonel R.S. McLaughlin, who reserved a special room for their display. It was always his wish that the paintings should never be separated. By giving them to the McMichael Canadian Collection, he was assured that they would remain together in perpetuity.

Clarence Gagnon first visited his favourite St. Lawrence painting site, Baie Saint Paul at the turn of the century, in 1900. There, he discovered his favourite themes of pastel-hued village streets, wayside shrines and parish churches. The quiet, rustic life of that early period finds its reflection in Gagnon's brush through the *habitant* figures at work, baking bread at open ovens, riding ox-pulled sleds or weaving on the doorsteps of their cottages. For the rest of his life, whether living in Quebec or Europe, Gagnon sustained his interest in the rural life of the lower St. Lawrence and Laurentians. Just before his death, he devoted his days toward a project to build a French-Canadian village museum to perpetuate the image of early habitant life.

Gagnon's great gifts as a painter have frequently overshadowed his abilities as a graphic artist. His series of etchings achieved during the first decade of this century are probably the finest ever done in this country. He also realized many distinguished figure drawings in the media of pencil and pastel.

Gagnon always carried his native Quebec within him wherever he travelled. Some of his best Canadian landscapes were painted in his Paris studio from sketches made at home. When he visited Norway or Switzerland, it was usually to sketch the snow which formed so much a part of his studies of scenes from his native land.

MARIA CHAPDELAINE

Maria Chapdelaine by the French author and journalist, Louis Hémon, is the classic novel of French Canadian *habitant* life. First published in 1914, the year after Hémon's death, it is unquestionably the most illustrated of all books about Canada. More than a dozen artists have decorated various editions including such distinguished Canadians as Suzor-Côté and Thoreau MacDonald.

The most famous edition of *Maria Chapdelaine* is that illustrated by Clarence Gagnon and published in 1933 by the Paris publishing house of Mornay. This volume is now one of the most sought-after of all books relating to Canada. It was first issued in a numbered deluxe edition of 2,000 copies, of which the McMichael Canadian Collection displays number 1545.

The 54 original illustrations for *Maria Chapdelaine* were presented by the late R. S. McLaughlin to the McMichael Canadian Collection and now form one of its most treasured exhibits.

... a paradise must it be this country to the South
... quels paradis ce devaient être ces contrées du sud

... some peculiar quality of sweetness and peace in that house in the woods.
... ces gestes ... revêtaient de douceur cette maison isolée dans les bois.

... "we have only dogs to draw our sleds, fine strong dogs ..."
... on n'a que des chiens pour atteler aux traineaux, de beaux chiens forts ...

... and chest against the bar, threw all their weight upon it ...
... et pesaient de toute leur force, la poitrine appuyé sur la barre de bois.

. . . the moment for laying wood is also that of the slaughtering.
. . . l'époque où l'on empile le bois est aussi celle où l'on "fait boucherie".

. . . were she to marry a man like Eutrope and accept a life of rude toil.
. . . ce qui l'attendait si elle l'épousait . . . une vie de labeur grossier . . .

. . . mosquitoes rose in swarms from the cut hay, tormenting the workers . . .
. . . les mouches et les maringouins les harcelaient de leurs piqûres.

. . . from dawn until nightfall, spending all strength in heavy tasks.
. . . du matin au soir, elle faisait le ménage et l'ordinaire . . .

... while the priest performed the sacred rites ...
... pendant que le prêtre accomplissait les gestes consacrés ...

... the two men took the double-handed saw, and sawed, and sawed.
... les deux hommes prirent le "godendard" et scièrent, scièrent, scièrent ...

... at every fall where logs jam and pile, would be found the river-drivers.
... à toutes les chutes, il faut encore le concours des draveurs forts.

... I will marry you as you asked me to ... in the Spring after this Spring ..."
... je vous marierai, le printemps d'après ce printemps-ci ...

EMILY CARR 1871-1945

Few artists have wedded nature and the human spirit so passionately as Emily Carr. A headlong, single-minded mingling of art with her love for her native British Columbia produced the finest expressionist painting Canada has known.

Emily Carr's long career was plagued by difficulties, financial and otherwise. Her creative demands upon herself, a lack of public appreciation and the pressures of poverty pursued her throughout her lifetime. She was forced to run a boarding house and make souvenir pottery to survive. For years, she was without the sustenance to paint. Despite this, with the encouragement of a few friends such as Lawren Harris, she persisted to create many masterpieces which include some of the most loved canvases in the history of Canadian art.

Emily Carr's first important works were closely related to the life and lore of the West Coast Indians. She spent much time among them, and from their totems, graveyards and churches composed some of her most dramatic paintings. Her canvases of the early 1912 series record such Indian villages as Skidigate, Tanov, Gitwangak and Alert Bay. In them, survive the houses, poles and people of an era then vanishing, as the career of Emily Carr was to cease for a period shortly afterwards. When she began painting again in the 1920's, Emily Carr was to approach the Indian material in a different mood and style.

By now, she was more concerned in capturing the spirit of the Indian structures than in recording them log by log. She simplified the totem poles and house poles, with their surrounding landscape, into abstracted designs which echoed the rich, carved rhythms of the Indian art itself.

By the 1930's, Emily Carr's attention turned almost completely to the B.C. coastal shorelines and forests. Her design-sense learned from the Indians and Cezanne found a looser expression. Her skies, earth and foliage became joined into a single swirling whole, reflecting her subjective feeling about her themes rather than their material facts.

Emily Carr's career as an artist spanned almost a half a century. Her earliest works are reticent watercolours done following studies in San Francisco and London. Her true power of expression first emerges in a series of brilliantly coloured canvases in the *fauve* manner painted in Brittany, France from 1910 to 1912. Upon her return to Canada in 1912, Emily Carr adapted the rich fauve style to portrayals of West Coast Indian villages and landscapes. Two examples of her work in this manner in the McMichael Canadian Collection are *Brittany, France* 1911 and *House And Garden*, probably painted in 1912.

By the early 1930's, Emily Carr had already achieved such familiar masterpieces as *Indian Church*, exhibited in 1933 by the Canadian Group of Painters. Her compelling and mystical wood interiors were also attracting the attention of a few discriminating collectors. The National Gallery of Canada had already purchased her west coast studies as early as 1928 and continued to do so through the 1930's and after. In the McMichael Collection the magnificent landscapes of the 1930's are represented by such superb, rhythmic compositions as *Reforestation* 1936, *Shoreline* 1936, *Old Tree At Dark* 1936 and *Edge Of The Forest* c. 1935.

Although she lived mostly alone, Emily Carr created a pictorial universe for others. From a caravan, in which she travelled up and down the British Columbia coast, she created an ageless art of the spirit to be shared by future Canadians for countless generations.

Emily Carr was a gifted writer and much of her life story and philosophy is to be found in such remarkable autobiographical books as *Klee Wyck*, *Growing Pains*, *House Of All Sorts* and *Hundreds And Thousands*.

Haida Village. c. 1930
83.2 x 60.9

Edge of the Forest. c. 1935
83.8 x 55.9

Brittany, France. 1911
46.8 x 61.8

Swaying. 1936
35.6 x 45.7

Old Tree at Dark. c. 1936
111.8 x 68.6

Corner of Kitwancool Village. c. 1912
111.1 x 68.6

Shoreline. 1936
68.6 x 111.7

New Growth. c. 1936
46.4 x 65.1

Reforestation. 1936
111.7 x 68.6

Haytime, Knowlton Quebec. c. 1930
56.7 x 67.0

ALBERT ROBINSON

1881-1956

The career of Albert H. Robinson was beset and shortened by illness. Rheumatism crippled him during the last decades of his life and his painting career was limited to a span of little more than twenty years. In that time, he produced some of the most subtle colour compositions ever painted of the Canadian landscape. The very earliest of these were of subjects in Europe, where he painted with his close friend A. Y. Jackson in Brittany in 1911. The delicate hues he favoured then were transferred permanently to the Quebec scene in the group of sketches and canvases he painted during the 1920's. These views of such areas as the Laurentians, Baie Saint-Paul, Saint-Fidele and Murray Bay are among the best loved and most sought-after views of French Canada.

Loosely rendered, in an almost patch-work technique of square edged, lozenge-shaped strokes, they represent a gentle and poetic response to the Canadian landscape. Robinson was primarily a painter of winter, but there appears no bitterness, starkness or challenge in his snow-clad hills and villages. His was a pastel vision. It is as though his pink, grey and blue dipped brush removed the severity from the land and left behind only the silver sunlight and the sound of sleigh bells. Like the happy French master, Raoul Dufy, Robinson turned almost everything he painted into a land a little gayer than the reality we see. Robinson's gentle tonal art is represented in the McMichael Canadian Collection by four canvases, including *St. Joseph* with its sapphire-like patches of water and several sketches of the villages he was so fond of recording.

Afternoon, Saint Simeon. c. 1924
56.0 x 66.5

J.W. MORRICE 1865-1924

J.W. Morrice was one of the gypsies of Canadian art. Born in Montreal, his wanderlust career took him among other places to Paris, Venice, Brittany, Spain, North Africa, Tunis, England, Cuba and Trinidad. Originally intended for a career at law, he first began to paint in the Toronto area while studying at the University of Toronto. Immediately upon finishing his legal studies, he headed for Paris to study art. For most of his life after that Paris remained his creative headquarters.

Morrice was a close friend of Canadian fellow-painters Maurice Cullen and William Brymner. Together, the trio had an immeasurable impact upon the country's art. Brymner taught A.Y. Jackson, Edwin Holgate, Clarence Gagnon, Helen McNicoll and many other important national painters. Both Morrice and Cullen were major influences upon such significant figures as A.Y. Jackson, Goodridge Roberts, Jacques de Tonnancour, John Lyman and Robert Pilot. Jackson often described Morrice and Cullen as the two who formed "the backbone" of his career.

Although he was an expatriate for most of his life, Morrice is one of the most popular and sought-after Canadian painters and is regarded by many, especially in Quebec, as our greatest painter. Certainly, Morrice has received the widest international recognition of any of our past artists. He was a close friend of the great French masters Henri Matisse and Albert Marquet, and the important British painter Matthew Smith,

and shared painting trips with all of them. Morrice's last late canvases, painted in the West Indies under the colour influence of Matisse are certainly among the best ever realized by a Canadian-born artist. Today, European critics agree that Morrice played a very real, if relatively minor role in the history of French art during the post-impressionist period.

Probably the most personal aspect of Morrice's art was his abbreviated drawing style. This loose, economic manner was already established as early as 1909 when he painted the famous *The Ferry, Quebec* and continues through to the last glowing Trinidad canvases.

Some of Morrice's most telling creations are the small pochades or quick sketches in oil he made in panels while sitting in city cafes or at the seashore. The seventeen examples of this type in the McMichael Canadian Collection reveal the artist's changing styles over a period of more than twenty years.

These range from an early grey, heavily painted panel *Notre Dame* to a luminous, simplified, sunlit view of *Tunis*, painted toward the end of his career. Although most of these works measure a mere four and three-quarters by six inches, each of them is a complete composition. The intimacy and warmth of these spontaneous notations puts them into a place of their own in Canadian art. The technique used to create these small oils was a combination of rubbed-in glazes and brushwork accents. Morrice carried a little sketchbox in his coat pocket and would stop to quickly record any on-the-spot scenes which appealed to him, whether they were in a country field or along a busy boulevard.

Although Morrice was restless in his travels, his painting arose from an inner creative constant. He turned natural forms to his own creative ends, regardless of whether he was in France, Quebec, North Africa, Cuba or Trinidad. His style of painting is unmistakable, regardless of theme.

Despite the influence upon him of several great artist-friends, Morrice remained his own creative man. There is a contagious charm about his art in general which is little short of pictorial magic. Morrice was a compulsive painter who recorded life from a deep love of the world around him.

Tunis. c. 1920-21
23.5 x 32.5

Sailboat. c. 1911
12.4 x 15.3

Algiers. c. 1919
25.0 x 23.5

Landscape in Trinidad. c. 1921
38.0 x 46.6

The Jetty. c. 1918
12.4 x 15.3

Along the Bank. c. 1909
12.3 x 15.2

Paris. c. 1909
12.3 x 15.3

Village Square. c. 1918
12.1 x 15.3

Indian Girl. 1932
76.3 x 61.0

Cobalt. 1928
26.5 x 33.8

YVONNE HOUSSER 1898-

Although Yvonne Housser was not a member of the Group of Seven she was closely associated with the movement and was a founding member of the Canadian Group of Painters which succeeded the original Group in 1933. In canvases painted in the late twenties and early thirties, she concentrated on portraying Northern Ontario mining towns. These studies vividly capture the special character of those isolated settlements, whose frame houses scattered on a sea of rock were among the most telling symbols of a desperate era in Canadian economic history.

The career of Yvonne Housser represents the restless, questing spirit of many artists born at the turn of this century. From a near-impressionist European style of the early twenties, she moved through a Group-oriented landscape period, a finely realized series of Indian portraits and Mexican scenes to the almost pure abstractions of the 1960's. Despite these changes from style to style, her evolution was a logical and organic one, and at no time do we find a change in direction for the mere sake of fashion.

Yvonne Housser taught at the Ontario College of Art for some thirty years and, like the creative teacher she was, continued her own studies under such international masters as Hans Hofmann at Cape Cod and Emil Bistram in Mexico. Her substantial body of paintings done over many decades represents only a part of her restless dedication to the creative life of Canada as artist, teacher and counsellor to many of her colleagues.

Autumn Forest. Mid 1930's
61.6 x 76.6

Slumber. Mid 1930's
82.2 x 102.5

Benedicta. c. 1932
184.0 x 122.4

RANDOLPH HEWTON—1888-1960

Randolph Hewton was one of the best trained of all Canadian painters. Beginning as a student under Montreal's famed William Brymner in 1903, he later studied and painted in Paris from 1908-1913. In Paris, Hewton shared his studio for a time with A. Y. Jackson, and the two painted together in rural France. Their joint exhibition of these European works held at the Art Association of Montreal in 1913 first brought Hewton and Jackson to public attention. Hewton later exhibited with the Group of Seven as an invited contributor. His art career was cut short when he decided to enter the business world in the early 1920's. Although he continued to paint some fine canvases—particularly of figure and portrait subjects—one can only guess what Hewton might have achieved if he had continued to concentrate upon his art.

Artist Unknown
Dark grey stone
27.4 x 19.8 x 5.5

Pauta
Cape Dorset
Grey stone
58.8 x 27.3 x 23.3

ESKIMO ART

One recent summer I had the great good fortune to visit Cape Dorset on Baffin Island, and sit with Pitseolak, many of whose fine prints are represented in The McMichael Canadian Collection, and talk with her about life.

She told me that she knew hers had been an unusual life. She was born in a skin tent, yet lived to hear on the radio that two men had landed on the moon. Like other Eskimo artists, with great veracity, she puts her life into her drawings. "I draw the old ways", she says, "the things we did long ago, and I draw the things I have never seen — the spirits and monsters". One day as we talked, she pointed to a print of hers of a tent in a book, and said to our young interpreter who, in blue jeans and modern gear, seemed to come from a very different world. "A long time ago, we used to live like that in the seal-skin tents — you wouldn't believe it, but it's really true!"

Eskimo artists detail for us, in a manner that surely seems "really true", home life in the tents and igloos, aspects of the hunt, childbirth, death, and the spectrum of Eskimo life. They record beliefs and legends, stories of true events, and, of course, they give us a marvelous diversity of animals and birds.

Most of the artists whose carvings and prints have so thrilled southerners over the last two and a half decades, lived, until recently, essentially the same kind of camp life that their ancestors knew for hundreds of years before them. There were some differences, of course. Most hunters killed with a gun, not bows and arrows; most Eskimos gained part of their livelihood from trapping, and traded fur bales for the white man's goods.

In this century most Eskimos are Christian, although Shamanism, the ancient religion of the hunting and gathering cultures whereby the world is ruled by spirit forces, still echoes in their lives. More than one shaman, the intermediary between the spirit forces and the community, has drawn his spirit helpers and put down his vision of the spirit world on paper. The shamanic content in some of the great prints undoubtedly represents the most eloquent statement of traditional Eskimo belief since Knud Rasmussen, the fluently bilingual Greenlander of Eskimo descent, published accounts of his talks with Eskimos, collected during his 1921-24 journey across Arctic America.

Certainly there is much to interest the anthropologist and students of different cultures in Eskimo sculpture and graphics. But perhaps there is more for the students of art.

It is not possible to miss the enormous vigor, the sure design, the elegance of form and execution which characterize Eskimo art at its best. At the same time, it is probably too soon for concensus to identify without possibility of error, the most important works and artists. For instance, the early prints from Povungnituk, sadly neglected at the time of their release, are only now beginning to receive the attention they deserve. But while much sorting out waits to be done — massive amounts of Eskimo art have reached the south — the universality of work commands our attention. One feels this, I think, in *Our Camp*, 1974 — Pitseolak's lyrical print of the Eskimo family asleep in the safety of their tent; one senses it too, in some of the strongly dramatic Baker Lake prints of Simon Tookoome. Graphics like *A Time of Plenty*, 1971, *A Vision of Animals*, 1973, though uniquely Eskimo in viewpoint, evoke celebration of the inter-relatedness of life and man's place in the animal kingdom. Here, in the south, far from the hunting fields, they remind us that man is a mammal.

What is the history of Eskimo art? Eskimo people first arrived in Arctic America several thousand years ago. They showed throughout the successive Eskimoan cultures that flourished on this continent, skill and craftsmanship in the manufacture of their tools and clothing. In addition, museums show us fine small carvings that may have had magical and religious significance. Later, in the 19th century, missionaries and anthropologists provided pencils and paper for drawing. Whalers and later the first traders were a market for ivory carvings.

Through the World War II years and immediately after, casual carving for the white man continued. Then in the late 1940's, the incident occurred which sparked the explosion of creativity that produced the sculpture and graphics now familiar to people around the world. The writer and artist James Houston, known to Eskimo people as 'Sowmik', brought back small Eskimo stone carvings from a sketching trip he made to Port Harrison in Arctic Quebec. Subsequently, a program to sponsor development of art in the North began. It was widely recognized that Eskimos needed a new source of income. The forces of change, sweeping in on Eskimo life during the first fifty years of the century, were proceeding with terrifying rapidity. For the first time, as Eskimo people put it, they had to "live with money." Out of this necessity has come an art of unexpected and remarkable quality.

The first contemporary sculpture to reach the south was followed by carvings from Baffin Island and by work from the western side of Hudson's Bay. Print-making experiments began in Cape Dorset in 1957, and today five communities send yearly editions of prints south. Both carvings and prints from the various Arctic communities tend to have distinctive styles recognizable to the practiced eye.

Houston's journeys resulted in the start of many artistic careers. In Cape Dorset his first visit there is remembered as an event of very great importance.

"I remember when Sowmik came to Cape Dorset and asked for carvings", the old man Noah told me one day. "Everyone was carving. Kiakshuk made a special snow shelter to do the work. I never saw Niviaksee carve, but later I heard he was really good at it. Sometimes Sowmik liked my carvings; sometimes he gave them back to me. But once he told my son, Napatchee, 'that's very good', and he gave him a .22".

The artist Lucy recalls, "We would draw our art down there in camp and when a dog team went to get supplies from Cape Dorset, we would take along these drawings and give them to Sowmik. Then we'd go back and do some more".

What does the future hold? This is a question that is often asked nowadays. Only a handful of Eskimos live full time on the land today. Since the middle 60's, settlements have effectively replaced camps, prefabs have replaced igloos, and all over the arctic children go to school. Eskimo people still like to be out on the land and many go whenever they can, especially in summer. However, the "old way" as Eskimos say, retreats now as the people who remember die. The content of the carving and prints is changing, faster in some communities than in others, and will continue to do so. There is great talent among young Eskimo people, but how they will employ it in the future, is a question that cannot be answered today. All we know for the moment is that Eskimos who knew and lived the old life have had the great ability to create out of their lives a magnificent record — a record we know instinctively, as Pitseolak says, is "really true".

Qumaluk
Povungnituk
Black stone
41.5 x 48.3 x 21.

148

150

A. Anaituq
Pelly Bay
Ivory on whalebone
3.7 x 9.9 x 5.4

Tiyeatsian
Repulse Bay
Ivory on stone
2.6 x 8.4 x 7.3

A. Anaituq
Pelly Bay
Ivory on stone
2.6 x 7.3 x 16.2

Unknown
Cape Dorset
Ivory on bone
3.1 x 4.4 x 2.2

Aqiggaaq
Baker Lake
Soapstone
25.0 x 26.5 x 33.0

Kiawak
Cape Dorset
Green stone
34.0 x 50.0 x 20.8

Henry
Soapstone
19.0 x 16.5 x 13.0

Peter Anowtok
Povungnituk
Black stone
56.3 x 44.3 x 42.7

151

Angrnasungaaq
Baker Lake
Soapstone
30.0 x 49.0 x 20.0

Barnabas Akkanarshook
Baker Lake
Soapstone
28.0 x 45.0 x 35.0

Davidee
Lake Harbour
Soapstone
40.5 x 17.0 x 25.5

The Hunters. 1962
Parr
Cape Dorset
74.0 x 53.0

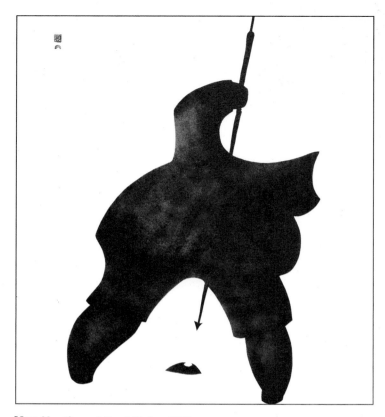

Man Hunting at Seal Hole. 1959
Stencil
Niviaksiak
Cape Dorset
59.7 x 44.8 (sight)

Woman in the Sun. 1960
Artist's Proof
Kenojuak
Cape Dorset
49.3 x 65.4

Umingmuk. 1973
Kananginak
Cape Dorset
58.0 x 78.3 (sight)

Our Camp. 1974
Pitseolak
Cape Dorset
72.8 x 57.6 (sight)

Tsimshian, Human Face Mask
Wood/paint
Carver Unknown
22.0 x 16.8 x 12.8

ART OF THE PACIFIC NORTHWEST COAST INDIAN

The Canadian art form best known to the rest of the world is that of our West Coast Indians. For almost a century, it has been rated internationally as one of the richest and most powerful of all tribal arts. As early as the late eighteenth century, Haida and Kwakiutl artifacts were finding their way into European collections.

Great forests provided the media for the majority of the Pacific northwest Indian artifacts. Cedar, fir and hemlock trees were transformed into masks, boats, totems, dwellings, utensils and clothes. The coastline supplied the sites for their villages, and the sea, generous provisions of food. Such a fortunate combination of circumstances enabled the coastal tribes to avoid the hazardous trips of their inland brothers and furnished ample leisure for lavish displays of boldly carved, decorated artifacts.

Their cultural area includes the entire coastline of British Columbia. The extreme generosity of the environment and the almost mystical atmosphere of the shrouded coast probably influenced the social and religious complexities which evolved with the first inhabitants. Supernatural creatures were basic to their concept of origin. The people created an art form which celebrated and communicated this belief while illustrating their lineal descent and providing a visual reminder of acquired privileges or rights. Status or prestige within the group was reinforced through the display of carved and painted paraphernalia.

The "potlatch" was the occasion for display when the dancers performed the origin myths wearing masks and costumes. Every conceivable object from small horn spoons to carved poles bore the totems or crests of the clan giving the feast. Generous gifts were given and if accepted, the guest recognized the ancestral and social claims of the giver whose nobility and status were thus enhanced.

Eight major tribal groups located along the coast are re-presented in The McMichael Canadian Collection. The Salish work differed significantly from that of the northern groups in artistic theme and style. The art was reflected in the costumes and adornments worn by the dancers to celebrate the guardian spirit myth.

The "Swaixwe" mask exemplifies the uniqueness of Coast Salish art with distinctive characteristics; bulging cylindrical eyes protrude as does the bulbous nose. Two birdhead horns surmount the head and backward pointing wooden spines are prominent on the splendid "Swaixwe" mask exhibited in The Collection.

The Nootka shared the northern belief that they were direct descendants of supernatural beings and claimed heraldic crests. Their decoration, in bold orange, blue and black, was often geometric and individual. The Nootka mask in The McMichael Collection, circa 1890, exhibits a downturned mouth.

The Kwakiutl perpetuated a complex system of secret societies each believed to have a mythical founder. In rituals and ceremonies dramatized during the winter months, dancers displayed large and complex masks often with movable parts which might reveal a mask face within. This dramatization of the idea of transformation was strengthened by the apparent possession of the dancers by supernaturals.

The "Hamatsa" or cannibal society was of major importance. The bird monsters "Hokhokw" (cracks open human skulls), "Kwakwakwalanooksiwae" (raven at the mouth of the river), and "Galodwudzuwis" (crooked beak of heaven), made their spectacular appearance as giant associates of the cannibal spirit. A fine Kwakiutl "Hamatsa" mask with a movable mouth may be seen in the gallery collection.

The Bella Coola were Salish migrants to the central coast of British Columbia. Their artists were motivated by a vision of the supernatural which was different from their neighbours, yet their masks rivalled those of the Kwakiutl. The dramatic carving of the Bella Coola is uniquely characterized by bulging features, heavy lines and a forceful use of colour, particularly a bright blue.

The McMichael Collection includes several Bella Coola masterpieces. The magnificent Bella Coola headdress figured prominently in ceremonies of the "Sisaok" society. A member was entitled to wear one or more weasel skins, and the nine skins on The Collection's headdress indicate the importance of the wearer. The "Sisaok" headdress is surmounted by up-turned grizzly bear claws and has abalone insets.

North of the Bella Coolas was a group of Kwakiutl people known as the Bella Bella. Their artistic style was a fine mix whereby influences of the dramatic south were balanced by northern refinements. Bella Bella art is considered, by some, to be the most exciting of the entire coast. The Collection's two Bella Bella face masks are circa 1890.

Tribes of the Tsimshian are distributed along the river valleys of the Skeena and Nass. A zenith in superbly carved frontal headdresses and portrait masks was achieved. The face, either human or animal, was often framed by minute, detailed faces or animals. Large spaces were left unpainted and colour, when used, was subtle.

The Queen Charlotte Islands and the southern tip of Alaska's Prince of Wales Island were the homeland regions of the Haida. Like the Tsimshian, sparing use was made of colour, but the scale of their poles was more monumental. Superb Haida human portrait masks were created, and a magnificent example in The McMichael Collection is Charles Edensaw's "Old Lady Wearing Labrette", circa 1880. The delicate movable eyelids are controlled by concealed strings.

Argillite carvings of miniature totem poles, human figure replicas, pipes and spoons are universally recognized Haida artifacts. Nineteenth century Haidas carved their familiar forms in argillite for trade goods. Decades later, splendid examples of this medium as an art form enhance the McMichael Western Canada room.

The greatest of the Haida carvers, Charles Edensaw (1839-1924), is represented in The Collection by an exquisite bracelet, beaten and carved from silver dollars, and by his beautiful argillite carvings. Each of his works is a masterpiece in concept and design. A superb example of Haida achievement may also be seen in the Raven Rattle originally collected in 1867, and now a part of The Collection.

West Coast Indian art was both religious and social. The giant totem poles were heraldic crests in which each chief boasted of his strengths and privileges. These were made visual by the use of such symbols as the beaver, bear, frog and killer whale. Of the many thousands of majestic poles commissioned by the chiefs for their villages, most have now decayed — victims of neglect, combined with time and weather. The splendid Willie Seaweed pole from Blunden Harbour was the last standing pole on the island, long deserted by the Kwakiutl people, following a change in their fishing patterns.

Not long ago, it seemed that the traditional art of the coast peoples might not survive. Cultural confrontation and direct suppression of the "potlatch" custom by federal authorities were profound obstacles. Perseverance, personified by the efforts of the late Mungo Martin, has led to a renewal of interest in this important facet of our cultural inheritance. Today there are growing numbers of fine artists who have schooled themselves in the coastal art tradition.

Doug Cranmer exhibits the strengths of his native heritage in his dramatically carved and painted lintels in the Western Canada gallery, together with his splendid adze-carved bench of British Columbia red cedar. Masterpieces like the gold box by the great Haida artist, Bill Reid, are contemporary and competently rival the art of old.

Bella Coola Sisaok Head-dress. 1924
Multiple media
Carver unknown
54.0 x 31.5 x 38.0

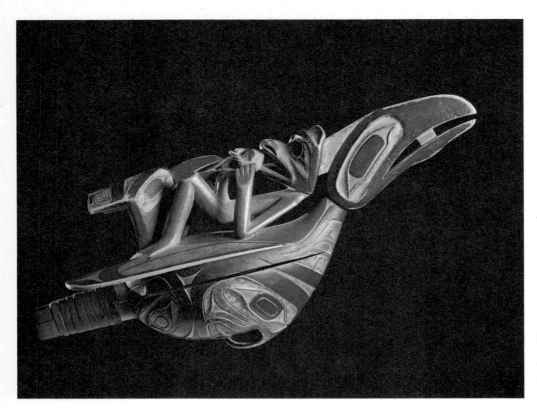

Haida, Raven Rattle.
c. 1825
Wood/paint
Carver unknown
11.0 x 31.7 x 10.3

Bella Coola, Thunderbird Mask
Wood/paint
Carver unknown
32.5 x 25.5 x 26.4

Kwakiutl Totem
Wood/paint
Willie Seaweed
650.0 x 43.0 x 36.0
The figures from the top down
Grizzly Bear
Thunderbird
Raven
Tsonoqua
Wasco

Kwakiutl, Komokwa Mask
Wood/paint/cedar bark
Carver Unknown
41.5 x 47.5 x 24.0

Haida, Argillite Figure
Carver Unknown
21.7 x 5.8 x 6.5

Haida, Argillite Pipe
Carver Unknown
21.5 x 6.7 x 2.0

Kwakiutl, Crooked Beak of the Sky Mask. c. 1880
Wood/paint/cedar bark
Carver Unknown
29.0 x 20.3 x 86.0

Kwakiutl, Komokwa Mask with Fish
Wood/paint
Carver Unknown
66.0 x 35.5 x 62.0

Kwakiutl, Raven Hamatsa Mask
Wood/paint/cedar bark
Carver Unknown
23.2 x 22.5 x 109.0

Haida Bracelet. c. 1910
Silver
Charles Edensaw
6.4 x 19.9 (cir.)

Argillite Totem
Charles Edensaw
16.5 x 3.4 x 4.6

Haida Frog Design Bracelet
Gold
Charles Edensaw
1.3 x 16.0 (cir.)

Argillite Totem
Charles Edensaw
16.4 x 3.5 x 3.0

Argillite Totem
Charles Edensaw
11.0 x 3.6 x 4.0

Artist's Wife and Daughter. 1975
Norval Morrisseau
101.6 x 81.3

WOODLAND INDIAN ART

Woodland Indian contemporary art takes us into a world where a people preserves and perpetuates ancient crafts, tells us of its legends and of its dreams, lets us share the diverse expressions of its view of the world, and proves the continuing vigour of its creative power. Since ancient times, everyday functional objects of the Woodland Indians have been shaped with a keen sense of beauty. Tools, canoes and clothing were decorated; porcupine quills were dyed and applied to hide and birchbark; birchbark was embellished with scraped patterns, and wood was carved with a superb sense of design. The objects of the spiritual life were even more lovingly designed. The secrets of Midéwewin society were recorded in drawings, often stylized, which transmitted myth and sacred practices from generation to generation. The medicine masks of the Iroquois were a renewed challenge to successive generations to express dream and tradition.

Early contact with settlers introduced new designs and brought trade goods which modified old methods of decorating. Glass beads were used for splendid and gloriously colourful geometric patterns which complemented and, to some extent, replaced porcupine quill decorations. Many of the traditional art forms are carried on to the present day. Contemporary descendants of Woodland Indians have revived some lost crafts and have taken them far beyond the original traditional limits. This is exemplified by the Mohawk pottery of Oliver and Elda Smith of Hagersville, who rediscovered the techniques and materials of this ancient art. There, the pottery wheel was, at first, the only western addition to the ancient practice.

Through contact with the Europeans, silver and silver work was introduced to the Iroquois craftsmen, but by the middle of our century, this art had declined and the tradition of craftsmanship had almost disappeared. Again, a contemporary generation of craftsmen returned to tribal design, and artists, like Elwood Green, reached new heights of achievement.

The medicine masks of the Iroquois are among the works which have been consistently maintained. Fine carvings by J. Thomas, 53, and T. Harris, 83, exemplify the work of two generations of Iroquois carvers. These masks should be seen in terms of the encounter between the creator and the headman of the false faces.

The creator met the giant false face leader who claimed that he was the maker of the earth. The creator challenged him to a contest — who could move the mountain? The great false face shook his turtle rattle and summoned the mountain, but the mountain moved only slightly. When the creator gave the command, the mountain obeyed and enormous heat was generated. The great false face turned his head. His face struck the mountain, breaking his nose, and his mouth became distorted by pain. As the heat of the mountain threatened to suffocate him, he struggled for air and his tongue was drooping. The creator told the great false face that he would give him a place in the rocky hills of the west, near the rim of the earth. He assigned him to the tasks of blowing sweet gentle air over the crops, driving disease from the earth and assisting hunters and travellers.

In the last decade, a new sculptural medium, a brown stone, steatite, has been introduced by Duffy Wilson, an Iroquois (Tuscarora). In his masterful hands, it tells us of the history and legends of the Iroquois Federation. Younger artists in Oshwekin have used this new medium to advantage.

In the 1960's, an entirely new artistic development occurred in northern Ontario. Norval Morrisseau, born at Fort William, began to paint the legends of his people. He first used black ink on brown paper, depicting the spirits and their interaction with man. Later, the subject widened into images which dealt not only with myth, but also with his view of the prehistory of his people, the relation between man and fellow man, the place of man in nature, and his feelings about life. As the content of his paintings diversified, the use of colour became freer and a more important component of his composition. In the earliest works, tones of brown and green were used, but later, colours became bold, reminding us of stained glass windows or brilliantly coloured glass bead designs. The first attempts of Morrisseau to paint the sacred legends of his people were fiercely resisted by those who guarded the secrets of the Midéwewin society. However, Morrisseau persisted and as he developed his own capacity as a painter, the opposition to his work gradually declined. His influence on other native artists soon made itself felt.

Carl Ray, originally discouraged by the hostility which his drawings evoked among the leaders of his band at Sandy Lake, returned to his creative work and began to draw and paint his version of legends and of life. Ray developed into one of the most accomplished of Ontario's native graphic artists. Others of the same generation painted with a strong awareness of European schools of painting. Daphne Odjig Beavon had sketched as a child and had been imbued by her grandfather with the traditions of her people. She had travelled abroad and had finally synthesized a style and an approach which straddles two worlds, leaving her equally at home in both. Further south at Rama, Arthur Shilling had started to master impressionistic techniques and depict the faces of his people. He spent a brief period at the Ontario College of Art and although his technique is Western, Shilling's painting is Indian because he is Indian and deeply feels for his people.

The work of Morrisseau, Ray and others, began to exercise an influence all over northern Ontario. Young artists were inspired by the boldness with which the Indian spiritual heritage was set down. They began to find their own way and their own development within this framework. Saul Williams, of Round Lake, Roy Thomas of Long Lac, Joshim and Goyce Kakegamic of Red Lake, Benjamin Chee Chee of Temagami, and Sam Ashe of Pickle Lake were among those who developed their own creative personality and their own individualistic style. As their work developed, a distinctive school of Cree-Ojibwa-Odawa painting became discernable.

Further south on Manitoulin Island, the birthplace of Daphne Odjig Beavon and Francis Kagige, a group of young painters, still in high school, began to express themselves in drawings and paintings. Their artistic activities were a facet of their growing interest in their heritage, an aspect of self-discovery and a determination to preserve and recapture the essence of their Indian heritage. Foremost among them were Blake Debassige and Martin Panamick. The former working with bold, broad and visionary shapes, the latter with precise draughtsmanship and a love of nature. James Simon blends dream and reality and invents an imagery of animals and spirits. These three often paint with Randolph Trudeau and John Laford, forming a group which bodes well for the future of Ontario native painting.

In parallel with the growth of the Cree-Ojibwa-Odawa school, there developed a group of painters whose art blended modern western artistic discoveries with Indian heritage. Odjig Beavon and Shilling are two of those artists. Others include Alex Janvier, who invents imaginary maps of pure colours which are graceful abstractions, and Clifford Maracle who uses the techniques of the Fauves to tell us what it is like to be an Indian in this technological world.

As we stand in the Woodland Indian gallery, we are enraptured by colour and form. We see the ancient traditions of the Woodland Indians preserved by contemporary native artists; re-expressed by a second self-taught group, who has invented new forms of artistic communication, and by a third group who uses modern western art. They are artists with enormous vigor and creative power and we are richer for having brought them together.

Tribute to the Great Chiefs of the Past. 1975
Daphne Odjig
101.8 x 81.0

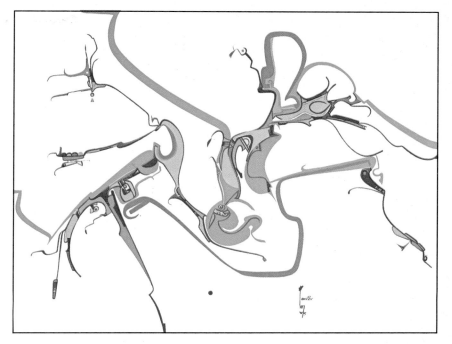

The Bureaucratic Supremist. 1975
Alex Janvier
56.0 x 71.3

Blue Indian Thinking. 1975
Clifford Maracle
122.1 x 122.1

Self-portrait. 1975
Arthur Shilling
84.0 x 61.4

165

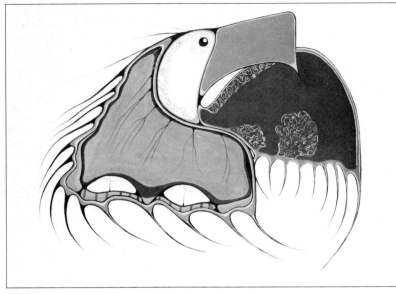

Thunderer Spirit. 1975
James Simon
76.0 x 91.3

Sacred Mide Bear and Loon Totem. 1975
Norval Morrisseau
76.2 x 101.5

Frolicking Loons. 1975
Carl Ray
55.9 x 76.2

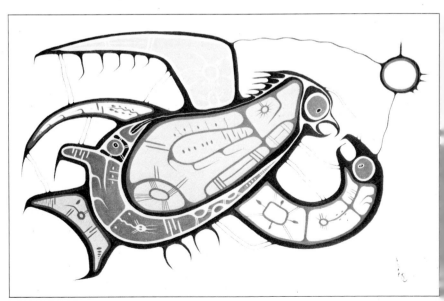

**Thunderbird, Demon Fish,
Lightning Snake.** 1974
Roy Thomas
56.0 x 84.0

To do da ho. 1975
Stone
Duffy Wilson
14.0 x 19.5 x 11.0

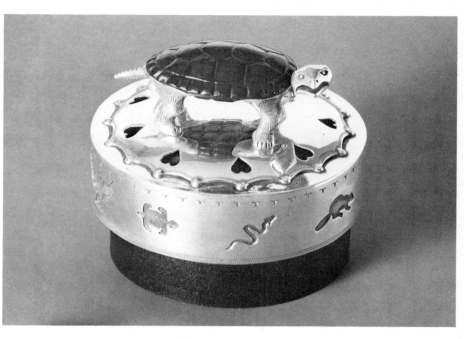

Symbolic Sculpture
Silver/stone
Elwood L. Green
7.4 x 11.3 dia.

Eagle Dancer Doll. 1975
Multiple media
Isobel Skye
51.5 x 84.0 x 29.0

Broken Nose Mask. 1975
Wood/paint/copper/horse hair
Jacob E. Thomas
27.0 x 23.0 x 12.5 (carving)

The Legend of the Crystal Bear. 1972
Stone/abalone shell
Joseph R. Jacobs
25.7 x 21.5 x 28.2

All measurements are in cm; height precedes width. Three dimensional objects are measured height, width, depth.

All paintings are oil on canvas or panel unless otherwise noted.

SIR FREDERICK BANTING.
1891-1941
Arctic Coast. 1926
21.7 x 26.7
Ellesmere Island. 1927
21.6 x 26.7
J. W. BEATTY. 1869-1941
The Red Roof. 1917
21.5 x 26.7
Country Lane. 1924
35.9 x 43.2

Winter Hills. c. 1925
21.6 x 26.7
FRANK CARMICHAEL.
1890-1945
Rocks and Stream. 1909
pencil
27.9 x 21.0
Go Home Bay. 1916
21.6 x 26.7
Hilltop Cedars. 1920
25.0 x 30.4

Autumn Tapestry. 1920
25.4 x 30.5
October Gold. 1922
120.0 x 98.7
Autumn Woods. c. 1922
24.6 x 30.4
Bolton Hills. c. 1922
24.6 x 30.2

Dead Spruce. 1922
24.7 x 30.2
Scarlet Hilltop. 1922
24.6 x 30.2
Tumbling Water. 1924
watercolour
21.5 x 26.3 (sight)
Clouds and Sunburst. 1925
25.4 x 30.5

Autumn, Orillia. 1926
25.0 x 30.3
Elms. 1928
pencil
20.6 x 26.8 (sight)
Lake Superior. 1928
25.5 x 30.5
Spring Garland. c. 1928
25.4 x 30.2

FRANK CARMICHAEL (cont.)
Summer Storm. 1928
103.0 x 123.0

Mirror Lake. 1929
watercolour
44.6 x 54.3 (sight)

A Northern Silver Mine. 1930
101.6 x 121.9

Farm House. 1930
pencil
20.7 x 26.8

Old Saw Mills, Severn Bridge. 1930
watercolour
58.4 x 74.8 (sight)

Old Store. 1930
watercolour
8.9 x 12.1

Bay of Islands. 1931
102.0 x 122.2

Northern Tundra. 1931
76.2 x 91.4

Church and Houses at Bisset.
c. 1931
25.2 x 30.4

Grace Lake. 1933
watercolour
27.8 x 32.8 (sight)

Cranberry Lake. 1934
pencil
20.6 x 26.8 (sight)

La Cloche Lake. 1934
pencil
20.8 x 26.8 (sight)

La Cloche Mountain Tops. 1934
pencil
20.5 x 26.9 (sight)

North of Lake Huron. c. 1934
30.2 x 40.6

Scrub Oaks and Maples. 1935
60.5 x 78.5

Hilltops. 1936
75.6 x 91.4

Alman's Trail. 1939
25.2 x 30.3

La Cloche Panorama. 1939
25.4 x 30.5

La Cloche Silhouette. 1939
25.5 x 30.5

Twisted Pine. 1939
25.2 x 30.5

Waterfall. 1943
tempera
72.9 x 98.1

EMILY CARR. 1871-1945
Brittany, France. 1911
46.8 x 61.8

Kispiox. 1912
62.2 x 30.5

Totem Pole. c. 1912
68.6 x 35.9

MILY CARR (cont.)
arden, Victoria. c. 1912
8.1 x 45.7

itseyucla. 1928
atercolour
4.0 x 40.0 (sight)

orner of Kitwancool Village.
1930
11.5 x 68.0

Haida Village. c. 1930
3.2 x 60.9

Sand Dunes and Mountains. 1933
oil on paper
54.6 x 89.5

The Mountain. 1933
112.0 x 68.5

Edge of the Forest. c. 1935
oil on paper
83.8 x 55.9

Old Tree at Dark. c. 1936
111.8 x 68.6

Straits of Juan de Fuca. c. 1936
oil on paper
60.9 x 91.4

Swaying. 1936
35.6 x 45.7

New Growth. c. 1936
46.4 x 65.1

Reforestation. 1936
111.7 x 68.6

Shoreline. 1936
68.6 x 111.7

Dancing Sunlight. c. 1937
82.8 x 59.8

Tree Forms. c. 1940
oil on paper
37.0 x 27.0

Dancing Trees. c. 1940
oil on paper
90.2 x 59.7

Forest. c. 1940
oil on paper
91.4 x 60.7

In a Wood. 1945
45.5 x 29.8

A. J. CASSON. 1898-
Nude Standing, Back View. 1917
pencil and wash
22.7 x 14.2 (sight)

Nude, Back View. 1917
pencil and wash
22.7 x 14.2 (sight)

Seated Nude. 1917
pencil
21.9 x 14.0 (sight)

A. J. CASSON (cont.)
Trees. 1920
24.6 x 28.6

Rock and Sky. 1921
23.6 x 28.6

Haliburton Woods. 1924
25.5 x 30.5

Summer Landscape. 1924
25.4 x 30.5

Poplars. 1925
25.0 x 29.6

Lake Rosseau. 1926
watercolour
26.7 x 29.2

Rocks and Clouds. 1926
linoleum block print
20.1 x 20.1 (sight)

Winter on the Don. 1926
watercolour
43.0 x 51.5 (sight)

Saturday Afternoon. 1927
watercolour
42.3 x 58.0 (sight)

Casson-Carmichael Camp. 1928
pencil
19.5 x 26.6 (sight)

Country Store. 1928
pencil
20.4 x 25.8 (sight)

Galt Road. 1928
pencil
19.8 x 26.6 (sight)

Hillsburg. 1928
pencil
19.7 x 26.7

Ice House, Port Coldwell. 1928
pencil
18.6 x 24.8 (sight)

Nashville House. 1928
pencil
20.5 x 25.8 (sight)

Sombreland, Lake Superior. 1928
23.7 x 28.3

Farmhouse, Salem. 1929
pencil
19.8 x 26.5 (sight)

Fog Clearing. 1929
watercolour
43.0 x 50.8 (sight)

Norval. 1929
25.1 x 29.1

Pike Lake. 1929
watercolour
42.2 x 50.7(sight)

Pinegrove Village. 1929
watercolour
23.8 x 27.3

Kleinburg. c. 1929
23.9 x 28.5

Old Man in Rocker. c. 1930
28.6 x 23.9

Thistletown, Late Winter. 193
pencil
20.0 x 26.2 (sight)

Spring, Lasky. 1932
watercolour
36.0 x 41.3 (sight)

A. J. CASSON (cont.)
Old House, Parry Sound. c. 1932
23.8 x 28.7

Church and Graveyard. 1933
21.6 x 26.7

Lake Baptiste. 1935
pencil
19.7 x 26.5 (sight)

Millworkers' Boarding House. 1935
23.7 x 28.4

Old House. 1935
watercolour
4.5 x 6.4

Rapids and Rocks. 1935
23.5 x 28.6

Flaming Autumn. 1936
25.0 x 29.8

Algonquin Park. 1940
pencil
16.4 x 19.0 (sight)

West Gilford. 1940
pencil
15.5 x 25.3 (sight)

Maple. 1941
pencil
19.7 x 26.7

McCrea's Mill, Lake of Two Rivers,
Algonquin Park. 1942
23.9 x 28.5

Fisherman's Point. 1943
tempera
76.0 x 101.1

Lake of Two Rivers. 1944
24.1 x 28.6

Summer Hillside, Kamaniskeg.
1945
50.8 x 60.9

Birch Island. 1945
24.0 x 28.6

A. J. CASSON (cont.)
Driftwood, Lake Kamaniskeg. 1946
31.6 x 39.2

Hills at Madawaska. 1946
24.0 x 28.6

Picnic Island. 1948
28.6 x 33.9

Island, Lake La Pêche. 1951
24.0 x 28.7

Cliffs, Lake Mazinaw. 1952
watercolour
28.0 x 34.7 (sight)

Lake Mazinaw. 1952
watercolour
27.5 x 33.7 (sight)

Rocks and Waterfall. 1952
pencil
13.8 x 16.3 (sight)

Britt. 1955
pencil
17.9 x 18.9 (sight)

Houses, Bancroft. 1955
30.4 x 37.8

Village House. 1955
50.8 x 61.0

A. J. CASSON (cont.)
White Pine. 1957
76.2 x 101.6

Ontario Scenes. 1958-60
pencil
various sizes

Tom Thomson's Shack. 1962
31.1 x 38.1

Mountains, Scotland. 1963
watercolour
22.1 x 29.7 (sight)

Maynooth. 1965
24.0 x 28.8

174

The Tom Thomson Shack. 1970
pencil   19.5 x 26.7 (sight)

Gibralter Point, Joe Lake,
Algonquin Park. 1976
pencil   22.0 x 29.0 (sight)

Casson Lake. 1976
30.5 x 38.1

MAURICE CULLEN. 1866-1934
Brook in Winter. c. 1927
60.9 x 81.3

NICKOLA de GRANDMAISON.
1892-1978
Indian Brave
pastel   56.7 x 46.4 (sight)

Nootka Chief
pastel
29.2 x 24.0 (sight)

Sarcee Indian
60.3 x 50.2

Chief Body
pastel
56.4 x 42.5 (sight)

William Twin
pastel
55.7 x 41.6 (sight)

Indian Woman
pastel
44.4 x 34.1 (sight)

Untitled
60.9 x 50.8

Blackfoot Papoose
pastel
34.3 x 26.6 (sight)

LIONEL LEMOINE FITZGERALD.
1890-1956
Trees in the Field. 1918
61.0 x 56.0

Prairie. 1921
18.2 x 22.1

Prairie Fence. 1921
16.9 x 22.2

The Harvester. 1921
69.0 x 62.2

Trees and Wildflowers. 1922
pastel
46.0 x 65.4 (sight)

The Cupola. 1924
27.9 x 27.9

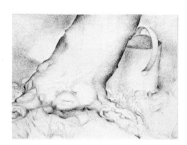

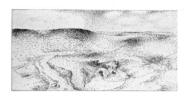

LIONEL LEMOINE FITZGERALD (cont.)
The Embrace. c. 1925
28.0 x 33.8

The Woods. 1929
pencil
24.0 x 30.1 (sight)

Williamson's House. 1933
153.7 x 111.8

Old Buildings and Shack. 1934
pencil
36.3 x 30.4 (sight)

Storm on Prairies. 1935
pencil
22.1 x 29.4 (sight)

Geraniums and Trees. 1935
pencil
31.1 x 20.8 (sight)

Tree Trunk. 1939
pencil
28.3 x 37.1 (sight)

Cliffs. 1944
pastel
58.2 x 43.0 (sight)

The Little Plant. 1947
60.9 x 46.4

Apple Basket. 1948
ink   29.6 x 45.8 (sight)

Trees. 1948
ink   28.3 x 19.9 (sight)

Oak Bluff. 1950
watercolour   26.7 x 37.4 (sight)

Prairie Landscape. 1955
ink   22.6 x 42.6 (sight)

CLARENCE A. GAGNON.
1881-1942
Twilight, Baie St. Paul. c. 1920
49.0 x 64.2 (sight)

Gagnon spent five years (1928-1933) lovingly portraying Quebec pioneer life in fifty-four superbly executed originals to illustrate Louis Hémon's Canadian classic "Maria Chapdelaine".

Mixed media on paper
 C.G. 1   7.3 x 7.9
 C.G. 2   15.5 x 22.6
 C.G. 3   17.0 x 21.8
 C.G. 4   20.6 x 21.1
 C.G. 5   18.0 x 18.9

C.G. 6   18.4 x 17.6
C.G. 7   16.1 x 22.0
C.G. 8   19.1 x 22.4
C.G. 9   22.1 x 23.4
C.G. 10   18.7 x 18.4

175

CLARENCE A. GAGNON (cont.)

C.G. 11	17.7 x 23.9	
C.G. 12	17.8 x 21.6	
C.G. 13	20.0 x 18.1	
C.G. 14	19.4 x 20.6	
C.G. 15	15.6 x 22.6	
C.G. 16	19.9 x 21.6	
C.G. 17	21.1 x 21.3	
C.G. 18	20.4 x 20.7	
C.G. 19	15.6 x 22.7	
C.G. 20	20.5 x 21.0	
C.G. 21	21.2 x 22.9	
C.G. 22	17.7 x 19.7	
C.G. 23	15.5 x 21.3	
C.G. 24	19.0 x 20.4	
C.G. 25	19.1 x 20.4	
C.G. 26	16.5 x 23.4	
C.G. 27	21.2 x 18.9	
C.G. 28	15.7 x 22.4	
C.G. 29	17.7 x 20.0	
C.G. 30	19.0 x 19.3	
C.G. 31	18.8 x 22.0	
C.G. 32	17.4 x 24.4	
C.G. 33	17.5 x 20.1	
C.G. 34	17.9 x 21.5	
C.G. 35	15.7 x 22.6	

CLARENCE A. GAGNON (cont.)

C.G. 36	17.6 x 21.4	C.G. 41	20.0 x 19.2	C.G. 46	17.7 x 19.5	C.G. 51	21.9 x 22.0
C.G. 37	18.7 x 21.6	C.G. 42	20.7 x 20.3	C.G. 47	19.4 x 22.0	C.G. 52	20.9 x 21.0
C.G. 38	15.6 x 22.8	C.G. 43	15.5 x 21.5	C.G. 48	19.5 x 20.8	C.G. 53	19.1 x 19.2
C.G. 39	20.0 x 19.4	C.G. 44	19.9 x 19.5	C.G. 49	19.5 x 20.3	C.G. 54	21.0 x 22.0
C.G. 40	17.4 x 23.8	C.G. 45	20.3 x 26.2	C.G. 50	16.9 x 25.8		

LAWREN HARRIS. 1885-1970
Rocky Brook. 1910
13.9 x 22.0

Little House. 1911
19.9 x 14.2

Old Mill. c. 1911
25.4 x 20.4

Algonquin Park Sunburst. 1912
20.3 x 23.5

Laurentians. 1912
14.0 x 21.8

Georgian Bay. c. 1912
13.9 x 21.8

LAWREN HARRIS (cont.)
Old Toronto Houses. 1912
pencil
22.5 x 17.4

Early Houses. 1913
26.9 x 33.5

Lake Simcoe. 1916
27.0 x 35.3

Kempenfelt Bay. 1916
26.9 x 35.3

Algonquin Park. 1917
35.3 x 27.1

Snow. c. 1917
71.2 x 110.5

Algoma Sketch. 1918
26.2 x 35.4

Sand Lake, Algoma. 1918
26.8 x 35.3

The Pool. 1918
26.7 x 35.3

Algoma Sketch. 1918
26.4 x 32.0

Algoma Sketch. 1918
26.7 x 32.0

Sunlit Hill. 1919
26.1 x 34.6

Algoma Reflections. 1919
26.4 x 35.1

Algoma Woodland. 1919
26.8 x 35.0

Still Water, Algoma. 1919
26.7 x 34.3

Beaver Dam. 1920
27.0 x 34.9

Montreal River. 1920
26.9 x 34.8

Red Maples. 1920
35.4 x 26.3

Quidi Vidi Gut, Newfoundland. 1921
26.7 x 35.2

Newfoundland Coast. 1921
26.8 x 34.9

Early House with Gateposts. 1921
pencil
19.5 x 25.0 (sight)

Early Houses with People. 1921
pencil
19.3 x 24.5 (sight)

Lake Superior Cliffs. 1921
30.2 x 38.0

Country North of Lake Superior.
1921
26.0 x 35.0

North East Lake Superior. 1921
26.7 x 34.6

178

LAWREN HARRIS (cont.)
Northern Lake, Autumn. 1921
30.6 x 38.1

Pic Island, Lake Superior. 1921
30.3 x 38.0

Louise Julia Holden. 1921
76.5 x 66.1

In the Ward. 1922
27.0 x 34.0

North Shore Panorama. 1922
26.3 x 35.3

Lake Superior Country. 1922
27.6 x 35.2

Shimmering Water, Algonquin Park.
1922
82.3 x 101.8

Algoma Canyon. 1923
30.1 x 37.8

Lake Superior Island. 1923
74.2 x 89.0

Pic Island. 1923
30.1 x 37.9

Pic Island. 1923
30.8 x 38.0

The Ice House. 1923
30.0 x 38.1

Northern Lake. c. 1923
82.7 x 103.0

Emerald Lake. 1924
30.4 x 37.9

Emerald Lake. 1924
30.4 x 37.9

Mount Temple. 1924
30.5 x 38.1

Mountain Sketch. 1924
30.3 x 38.0

Pic Island. 1924
121.9 x 152.4

Shore Rocks. 1924
30.2 x 37.8

Snow, Rocky Mountains. 1925
26.8 x 35.3

South End of Maligne Lake. 1925
27.0 x 35.2

Northern Lake. 1926
30.4 x 37.6

Lake and Mountains. 1927
30.3 x 38.0

Rocky Mountain Sketch,
Mt. Lefroy. c. 1928
30.5 x 38.1

Mountains and Lake. 1929
91.9 x 114.4

179

LAWREN HARRIS (cont)
Mt. Lefroy. c. 1929
30.5 x 38.1

Eclipse Sound and Bylot Island.
1930
30.2 x 38.0

Ellesmere Island. 1930
30.2 x 37.6

Icebergs, Davis Strait. 1930
121.9 x 152.4

Wareham Island, Cumberland Gulf,
Baffin Island. 1930
30.3 x 38.0

Preparatory Drawing for Mt. Lefroy.
1930
pencil
19.3 x 25.5

Mount Lefroy. 1930
132.7 x 153.3

Abstract Sketch. c. 1937
30.7 x 38.0

Maligne Lake. 1940
tempera
76.2 x 101.6

Autumn Rhythm. c. 1957
91.8 x 69.0

RANDOLPH HEWTON. 1888-1960
Après-Midi Camaret. 1913
73.0 x 60.6

Autumn Forest. c. 1935
61.6 x 76.6

Rocky Slopes. c. 1935
51.0 x 61.2

Slumber. c. 1935
82.2 x 102.5

Spring in the Valley. c. 1935
51.3 x 61.2

Benedicta. c. 1935
184.0 x 122.4

EDWIN HOLGATE. 1892-1977
Nude. 1922
29.2 x 25.4

The Cellist. 1923
129.5 x 97.8

Mother & Daughter. 1926
61.4 x 60.1

Fishermen's Houses. c. 1933
51.0 x 61.2

The Head. 1938
45.7 x 36.8

Melting Snow. 1948
21.6 x 27.0

Two Bathers. 1949
38.3 x 44.4

Hannah. 1957
50.6 x 50.3

A. Y. JACKSON (cont.)
Riverbank and Green Trees. 1914
21.5 x 26.8

The Red Maple. 1914
21.7 x 26.9

Cathedral at Ypres. 1917
21.7 x 26.8

Lorette Ridge. 1917
21.6 x 26.8

Agawa River. 1919
21.0 x 26.7

Algoma Canyon. 1919
27.0 x 21.4

Beaver Lake, Algoma. 1919
21.3 x 26.7

Beaver Pond in Autumn. 1919
21.2 x 26.4

Twisted Trees. 1919
21.0 x 26.8

Early Spring. 1920
21.2 x 26.5

Go Home Bay. 1920
20.2 x 26.8

Storm, Georgian Bay. c. 1920
21.6 x 26.6

First Snow, Algoma. c. 1920
107.4 x 127.7

Père Raquette. 1921
tempera
80.0 x 64.8

Waterfall, Algoma. 1921
21.6 x 26.7

Lake in the Hills. 1922
65.0 x 82.8

Dawn, Pine Island. 1923
53.0 x 65.0

October, Lake Superior. 1923
21.2 x 26.6

Quebec Houses and Sleigh. 1923
21.4 x 26.7

Murray Bay. c. 1923
21.4 x 26.8

Above Lake Superior. 1924
116.8 x 147.3

Pic Island, Lake Superior. 1925
21.6 x 26.7

Barns. 1926
21.6 x 26.7

Indian Home. 1926
21.1 x 26.6

Mountains near Skeena. 1926
21.5 x 26.8

A. Y. JACKSON (cont.)
Skeena Crossing. 1926
54.0 x 66.8

Totem Poles, Indian Village. 1926
21.6 x 26.7

Totems, Skeena River. 1926
21.6 x 26.7

Arctic Summer. 1927
pen
20.5 x 18.0 (sight)

Bic. 1927
21.6 x 26.7

Eskimo Summer Camp. 1927
51.0 x 64.1

Eskimos and Tent. 1927
21.5 x 26.8

Labrador. 1927
pen
20.5 x 18.1 (sight)

Mt. Rocher near Hazelton, B.C.
1927
21.1 x 26.7

Ice, Davis Strait. 1927
21.3 x 26.6

River, Baie St. Paul. 1928
21.4 x 26.7

Yellowknife Forest. 1928
21.3 x 26.7

Fishing Boats. c. 1928
21.4 x 26.9

Murray Bay. c. 1929
21.3 x 26.6

Grey Day, Hull, Quebec. 1930
21.4 x 26.7

Iceberg at Godhaven. 1930
21.1 x 26.7

River Road, Murray Bay. 1930
22.6 x 27.4

Morning, La Malbaie. 1930
20.5 x 26.7

Quebec Village. c. 1930
21.4 x 26.7

St. Tite des Caps. c. 1930
21.6 x 26.7

Church at St. Urbain. 1931
54.0 x 66.6

St. Joachim. 1932
21.5 x 26.6

Cobalt. 1932
21.5 x 26.5

Blue Water, Georgian Bay. c. 1932
21.4 x 26.7

Grey Day, Laurentians. 1933
54.0 x 66.2

183

A. Y. JACKSON (cont.)
St. Urbain. 1933
21.7 x 26.6

Les Éboulements, Quebec. 1933
21.4 x 26.7

Near Murray Bay. 1933
21.6 x 26.7

Nellie Lake. 1933
76.9 x 81.4

Quebec Village in Winter. 1933
21.2 x 26.7

Valley of the Gouffre River. 1933
64.5 x 82.2

Algoma November. 1934
26.5 x 34.7

Winter Morning, St. Tite des Caps.
1934
54.1 x 67.0

Houses, St. Urbain. c. 1934
21.6 x 26.7

Fishing Village, Gaspé Shore. 1934
26.7 x 34.2

Cobalt Mine Shaft. 1935
21.6 x 26.6

River St. Urbain. 1935
21.2 x 26.8

St. Lawrence at St. Fabien. 1935
21.4 x 26.7

Alberta Foothills. 1937
64.0 x 81.2

Radium Mine. 1938
82.0 x 102.7

Sunlit Tapestry. 1939
71.5 x 91.6

Quebec Farm. c. 1940
21.4 x 26.7

Tom Thomson's Shack. c. 1942
pencil
22.1 x 29.7 (sight)

St. Pierre. 1942
21.6 x 26.7

St. Pierre, Montmagny. 1942
21.6 x 26.7

Larch, Banff. 1944
26.7 x 34.3

Bent Pine. 1948
81.3 x 102.0

Late Morning, St. Aubert. c. 1948
26.7 x 34.3

Dogrib Indian Chief's Grave. 194?
53.6 x 66.4

Superstition Island, Great Bear
Lake. 1950
53.3 x 66.0

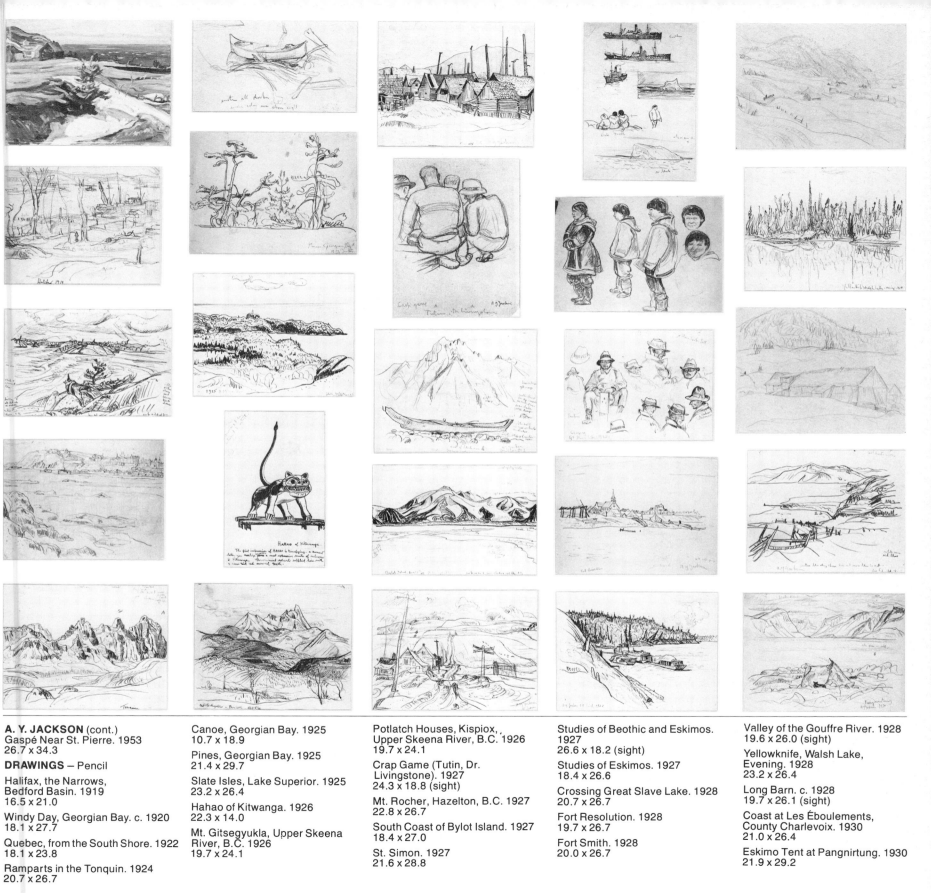

A. Y. JACKSON (cont.)
Gaspé Near St. Pierre. 1953
26.7 x 34.3

DRAWINGS – Pencil

Halifax, the Narrows,
Bedford Basin. 1919
16.5 x 21.0

Windy Day, Georgian Bay. c. 1920
18.1 x 27.7

Quebec, from the South Shore. 1922
18.1 x 23.8

Ramparts in the Tonquin. 1924
20.7 x 26.7

Canoe, Georgian Bay. 1925
10.7 x 18.9

Pines, Georgian Bay. 1925
21.4 x 29.7

Slate Isles, Lake Superior. 1925
23.2 x 26.4

Hahao of Kitwanga. 1926
22.3 x 14.0

Mt. Gitsegyukla, Upper Skeena
River, B.C. 1926
19.7 x 24.1

Potlatch Houses, Kispiox,
Upper Skeena River, B.C. 1926
19.7 x 24.1

Crap Game (Tutin, Dr.
Livingstone). 1927
24.3 x 18.8 (sight)

Mt. Rocher, Hazelton, B.C. 1927
22.8 x 26.7

South Coast of Bylot Island. 1927
18.4 x 27.0

St. Simon. 1927
21.6 x 28.8

Studies of Beothic and Eskimos.
1927
26.6 x 18.2 (sight)

Studies of Eskimos. 1927
18.4 x 26.6

Crossing Great Slave Lake. 1928
20.7 x 26.7

Fort Resolution. 1928
19.7 x 26.7

Fort Smith. 1928
20.0 x 26.7

Valley of the Gouffre River. 1928
19.6 x 26.0 (sight)

Yellowknife, Walsh Lake,
Evening. 1928
23.2 x 26.4

Long Barn. c. 1928
19.7 x 26.1 (sight)

Coast at Les Éboulements,
County Charlevoix. 1930
21.0 x 26.4

Eskimo Tent at Pangnirtung. 1930
21.9 x 29.2

185

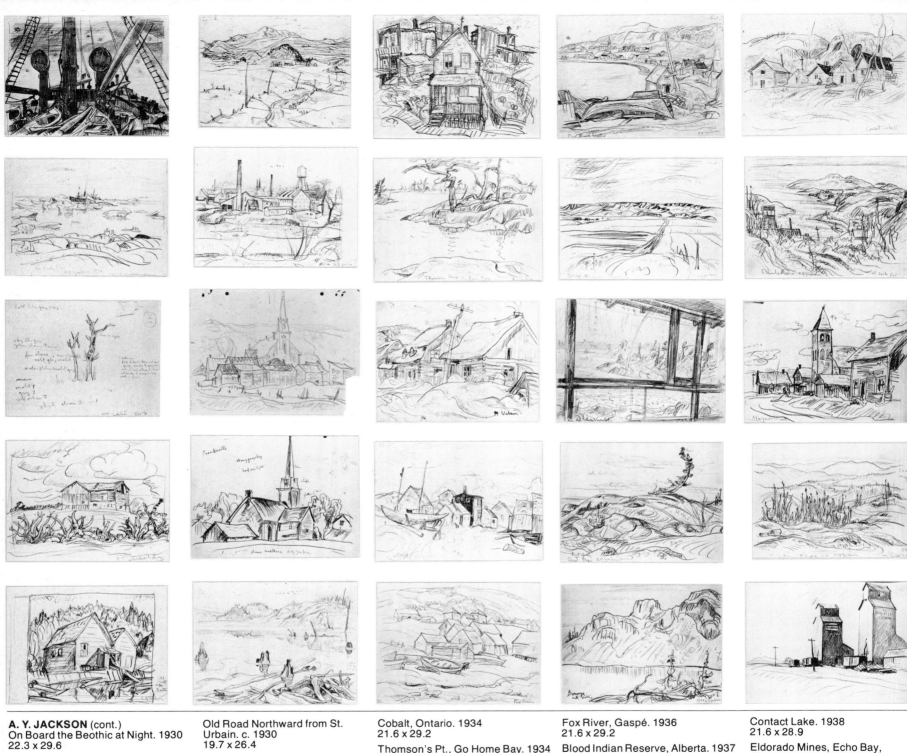

A. Y. JACKSON (cont.)
On Board the Beothic at Night. 1930
22.3 x 29.6

The Beothic off Bache Peninsula.
1930
21.6 x 28.8

Dead Tree Study, c. 1930
16.5 x 21.0

Old Barn near Caledon, Ontario.
c. 1930
22.8 x 26.4

Old Mill, Cape Breton Island. c. 1930
21.9 x 29.2

Old Road Northward from St.
Urbain. c. 1930
19.7 x 26.4

St. Hyacinthe on the Yamaska
River. c. 1930
21.9 x 29.2

Church at St. Urbain. c. 1930
19.5 x 26.0 (sight)

United Church at Frankville,
Ontario. 1932
21.9 x 29.6

Lake in Algoma East. 1933
22.3 x 29.6

Cobalt, Ontario. 1934
21.6 x 29.2

Thomson's Pt., Go Home Bay. 1934
21.9 x 29.2

Houses, St. Urbain. c. 1934
20.3 x 27.3

Fishing Village, Gaspé Shore. 1934
21.6 x 29.6

Fox River. 1936
21.4 x 28.7 (sight)

Fox River, Gaspé. 1936
21.6 x 29.2

Blood Indian Reserve, Alberta. 1937
21.9 x 28.6

Rain, McCallum's Veranda. 1937
21.9 x 29.6

Bent Spruce, Great Bear Lake. 1938
21.6 x 28.6

Coastline of Great Bear Lake. 1938
22.3 x 28.8

Contact Lake. 1938
21.6 x 28.9

Eldorado Mines, Echo Bay,
Great Bear Lake. 1938
21.6 x 28.6

Maynooth, Ontario. 1938
22.3 x 29.9

South from Great Bear Lake. 1938
21.6 x 28.8

Grain Elevators, Western Canada.
1940
21.6 x 28.8

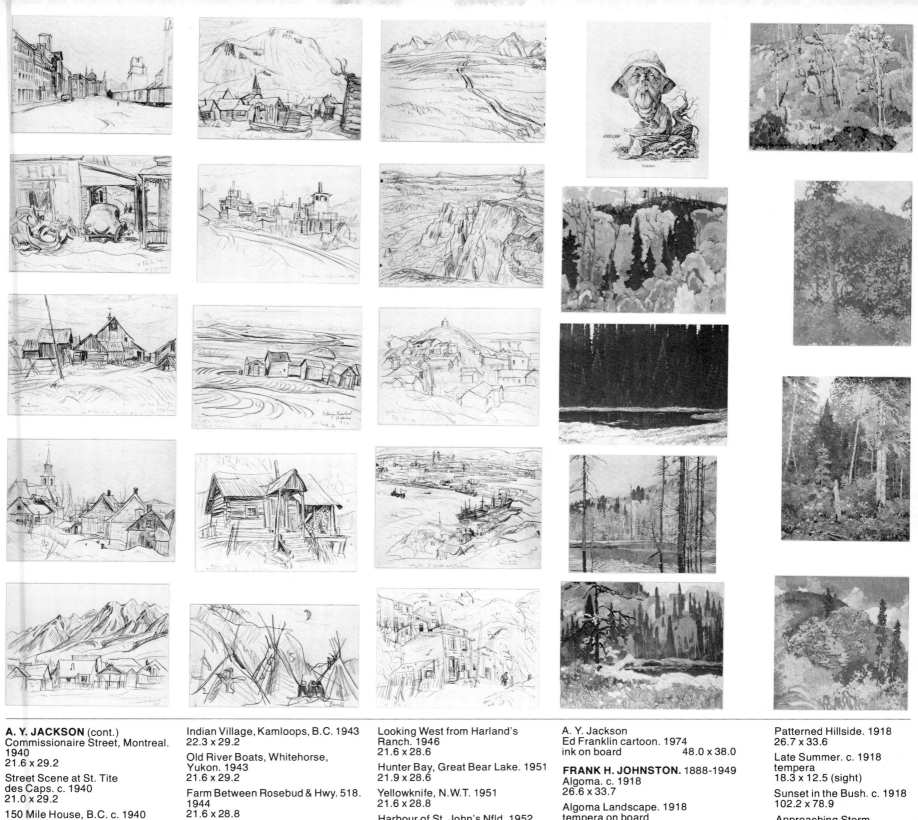

A. Y. JACKSON (cont.)
Commissionaire Street, Montreal.
1940
21.6 x 29.2

Street Scene at St. Tite
des Caps. c. 1940
21.0 x 29.2

150 Mile House, B.C. c. 1940
21.3 x 28.8

St. Pierre, County Montmagny. 1942
21.6 x 29.6

Canmore, Alberta. 1943
21.9 x 29.2

Indian Village, Kamloops, B.C. 1943
22.3 x 29.2

Old River Boats, Whitehorse,
Yukon. 1943
21.6 x 29.2

Farm Between Rosebud & Hwy. 518.
1944
21.6 x 28.8

Miner's Shack, Barkerville. 1945
22.3 x 29.2

Indian Tents, Banff. 1946
12.9 x 19.3(sight)

Looking West from Harland's
Ranch. 1946
21.6 x 28.6

Hunter Bay, Great Bear Lake. 1951
21.9 x 28.6

Yellowknife, N.W.T. 1951
21.6 x 28.8

Harbour of St. John's Nfld. 1952
21.6 x 29.2

Houses above St. John's Nfld. 1952
21.9 x 29.6

A. Y. Jackson
Ed Franklin cartoon. 1974
ink on board   48.0 x 38.0

FRANK H. JOHNSTON. 1888-1949
Algoma. c. 1918
26.6 x 33.7

Algoma Landscape. 1918
tempera on board
76.2 x 101.6

Drowned Land, Algoma. 1918
tempera   44.5 x 53.5 (sight)

Moose Pond. 1918
26.4 x 33.8

Patterned Hillside. 1918
26.7 x 33.6

Late Summer. c. 1918
tempera
18.3 x 12.5 (sight)

Sunset in the Bush. c. 1918
102.2 x 78.9

Approaching Storm,
Algoma. 1919
tempera on board
30.7 x 30.7

FRANK H. JOHNSTON (cont.)
Late Afternoon, Algoma. 1919
tempera on board
42.5 x 56.7

Dawn Silhouette. c. 1922
tempera   11.4 x 17.2

J. E. H. MacDonald. 1928
pen and ink
30.5 x 26.1

Winter Beauty. 1935
50.8 x 61.3

Debussy. c. 1945
50.5 x 61.0

ARTHUR LISMER. 1885-1969
Coastal Scene. 1904
watercolour
23.2 x 35.4 (sight)

Antwerp Harbour. 1907
26.4 x 37.8

Antwerp Harbour. 1907
30.3 x 39.1

An Ontario Landscape. 1911
30.3 x 39.4

J. E. H. MacDonald. 1912
pencil
17.7 x 14.5 (sight)

Tom Thomson. 1912
brush and ink
22.8 x 30.5

Tom Thomson at Grip. 1912
pencil
19.7 x 21.3

Algonquin Park. 1914
30.5 x 23.2

Tom Thomson's Camp. 1914
31.0 x 23.0

My Garden, Thornhill. 1916
36.4 x 52.0

Playtime. c. 1918
30.5 x 40.0

War Drawing. c. 1918
charcoal
30.0 x 41.0

Esther Lismer Reading. c. 1918
30.5 x 40.5

Georgian Bay Islands. 1920
30.5 x 40.3

Gusty Day, Georgian Bay. 1920
22.8 x 30.3

Rain in the North Country. 1920
22.2 x 30.8

Forest, Algoma. 1922
71.1 x 91.4

Sunset, Algoma. 1922
23.3 x 30.5

The Knockers' Table. 1922
pencil
46.4 x 76.2

Stormy Sky, Georgian Bay. 1922
30.3 x 40.4

ARTHUR LISMER (cont.)
In My Studio. 1924
60.8 x 76.2

Summer Day. 1924
41.0 x 50.8

Dead Tree, Georgian Bay. 1926
32.7 x 40.6

Preliminary Sketch, Evening
Silhouette. 1926
22.8 x 30.4

Evening Silhouette. 1926
32.5 x 40.5

Old Barn, Quebec. 1926
30.1 x 40.9

October on the North Shore. 1927
32.3 x 40.8

Lake Superior. 1927
32.3 x 40.1

Lake Superior Shoreline. 1927
32.1 x 40.9

Pines Against the Sky. 1929
29.9 x 40.6

Red Sapling. 1929
33.0 x 40.8

Maritime Village. 1930
30.5 x 36.8

Moon River, Georgian Bay. 1931
30.7 x 39.1

Georgian Bay Inlet. 1932
30.3 x 40.0

McGregor Bay. 1933
30.0 x 40.6

Pine and Rocks. 1933
30.5 x 39.4

Green Pool. 1935
30.4 x 40.2

Bright Land. 1938
83.0 x 103.0

Maritime Wharf. 1938
watercolour
42.6 x 57.7 (sight)

Pine Wrack. 1939
watercolour
54.6 x 76.2

Mother and Child. 1946
31.1 x 23.4

Canadian Jungle. c. 1946
45.8 x 54.6

Georgian Bay. 1947
29.2 x 39.4

Near Amanda, Georgian Bay. 1947
30.2 x 40.4

Still Life with Greek Head. 1949
30.2 x 40.3

ARTHUR LISMER (cont.)
Pine and Rock, Georgian Bay. 1950
30.4 x 40.3

Red Anchor. 1954
30.1 x 40.1

J.E.H. MacDONALD. 1873-1932
Nova Scotia. 1898
watercolour
23.6 x 12.1

In High Park. 1908
9.0 x 12.7

Oaks, October Morning. 1909
17.5 x 12.8

Snow, High Park. 1909
12.6 x 17.6

Thomson's Rapids, Magnetawan
River. 1910
15.2 x 23.4

Chipmunk Point. 1911
18.2 x 12.5

Laurentian Storm. 1913
11.4 x 11.4

Oakwood. 1913
20.4 x 25.3

On the Warpath. c. 1913
28.7 x 36.2 (sight)

Snow, Algonquin Park. 1914
20.2 x 25.3

Logs on the Gatineau River.
c. 1914
20.3 x 25.4

Sunflower Garden. 1915
20.3 x 25.3

Sunflower Study, Tangled
Garden Sketch. 1915
25.4 x 20.2

Storm Clouds. c. 1915
20.2 x 25.4

Gatineau River. c. 1916
20.2 x 25.4

Near Minden. 1916
20.3 x 25.4

Northern Lights. 1916
20.2 x 25.4

Wild Ducks. 1916
20.2 x 25.4

Harvest Evening. 1917
76.2 x 101.0

Canoe Lake. 1917
20.2 x 25.4

In November. 1917
53.2 x 66.0

Leaves in the Brook. 1918
21.3 x 26.6

Rocky Stream, Algoma. 191▪
21.3 x 26.5

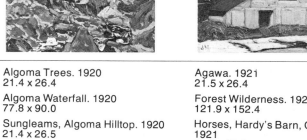

E. H. MacDONALD (cont.)
ung Maples, Algoma. 1918
.6 x 26.6

goma Bush, September. 1919
.4 x 26.6

eaver Dam and Birches. 1919
.5 x 26.5

ake in the Valley. 1919
.4 x 26.7

eaves in the Brook. 1919
.8 x 66.3

Silver Swamp, Algoma. 1919
21.4 x 26.6

Stormy Weather, Algoma. 1919
21.4 x 26.5

Agawa River, Algoma. 1919
21.6 x 26.6

Algoma Forest. 1919
21.4 x 26.5

Algoma Woodland. 1919
21.4 x 26.6

Algoma Hills. 1920
21.4 x 26.4

Autumn, Algoma. 1920
21.4 x 26.7

Moose Lake, Algoma. 1920
21.3 x 26.5

The Lake, Grey Day. 1920
21.4 x 26.5

Agawa Canyon. 1920
21.3 x 26.6

Algoma Trees. 1920
21.4 x 26.4

Algoma Waterfall. 1920
77.8 x 90.0

Sungleams, Algoma Hilltop. 1920
21.4 x 26.5

Tree Patterns. 1920
21.7 x 26.4

Woodland Brook. 1920
21.4 x 26.4

Agawa. 1921
21.5 x 26.4

Forest Wilderness. 1921
121.9 x 152.4

Horses, Hardy's Barn, Oakwood.
1921
21.7 x 26.6

Trees in Sea Mist. 1922
21.4 x 26.4

Nova Scotia Barn. 1922
10.8 x 12.7

191

J. E. H. MacDONALD (cont.)
Nova Scotian Shore. 1922
21.5 x 26.4

Buckwheat Field. 1923
21.3 x 26.4

Pastures, Gull River. 1923
21.6 x 26.7

Lake McArthur, Lake O'Hara
Camp. 1924
21.6 x 26.7

Autumn Sunset. 1925
pen and ink
24.2 x 28.5 (sight)

Lodge Interior, Lake O'Hara. 1925
21.4 x 26.6

Northern Pine. 1925
pen and ink
21.1 x 15.0 (sight)

Valley from McArthur Lake,
Rocky Mountains. 1925
17.7 x 22.8

Lake O'Hara and Mt. Lefroy. c. 1925
21.5 x 26.7

Prairie Sunrise. 1926
21.6 x 26.7

Snow, Lake O'Hara. 1926
21.6 x 26.7

Wiwaxy Peaks, Lake O'Hara. 1926
21.6 x 26.7

Artist's Home and Orchard. 1927
21.5 x 26.3

Cathedral Peak, Lake O'Hara. 1927
21.4 x 26.6

Cathedral Mountain. 1927
21.9 x 26.6

Little Turtle Lake. 1927
13.2 x 21.5

Snow, Lake O'Hara Camp. 1927
21.4 x 26.6

Lake O'Hara. 1928
21.4 x 26.7

Lake O'Hara, Rainy Weather. 1928
21.4 x 26.6

Above Lake O'Hara. 1929
21.6 x 26.7

Mountains and Larch. 1929
21.4 x 26.4

Storm Clouds, Mountains. 19
21.6 x 26.7

Tamarack, Lake O'Hara. 192
21.6 x 26.7

Lichen Covered Shale Slabs
21.4 x 26.6

Mountain Stream. 1930
21.4 x 26.6

192

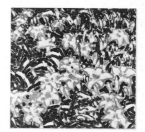

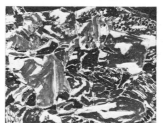

J. E. H. MacDONALD (cont.)
Aurora, Georgian Bay. 1931
21.5 x 26.7

Wheatfield, Thornhill. 1931
21.6 x 26.7

Goat Range, Rocky Mountains.
1932
53.8 x 66.0

THOREAU MacDONALD. 1901-
Old House. c. 1924
mixed media
14.8 x 18.5 (sight)

Book Jacket. 1926
pen and ink
24.2 x 16.9 (sight)

Marsh Hawk. 1939
50.8 x 76.2

St. John's, York Mills. 1940
pen and ink
15.2 x 17.8

Great Horned Owl. c. 1940
58.4 x 60.9

Squared Logs near Purpleville. 1950
pen and ink
14.0 x 17.5

Great Slave Lake. c. 1950
pen and ink
22.7 x 31.6 (sight)

Man and His Horse. 1965
pen and ink
9.0 x 9.5 (sight)

Tom Thomson. 1965
pen and ink
21.3 x 17.1

Canoe. 1969
pen and ink
15.2 x 22.8

Loon. 1969
pen and ink
15.2 x 22.8

Man and Canoe. 1969
pen and ink
10.1 x 21.6

DAVID B. MILNE. 1882-1953
Blue Interior. c. 1913
51.1 x 46.0

The Bronx. c. 1914
60.3 x 50.2

Patsy. 1914
51.7 x 61.7

Relaxation. 1914
tempera on paper
37.6 x 45.7

West Saugerties. 1914
51.2 x 43.2

The Lilies. 1914
50.7 x 50.7

Boston Corners. 1916
45.5 x 52.7

Blue Hills. 1917
tempera on paper
37.0 x 53.8 (sight)

Blue Church. 1920
46.8 x 56.7

Painting Hut, Christmas. 1920
watercolour
35.1 x 25.3 (sight)

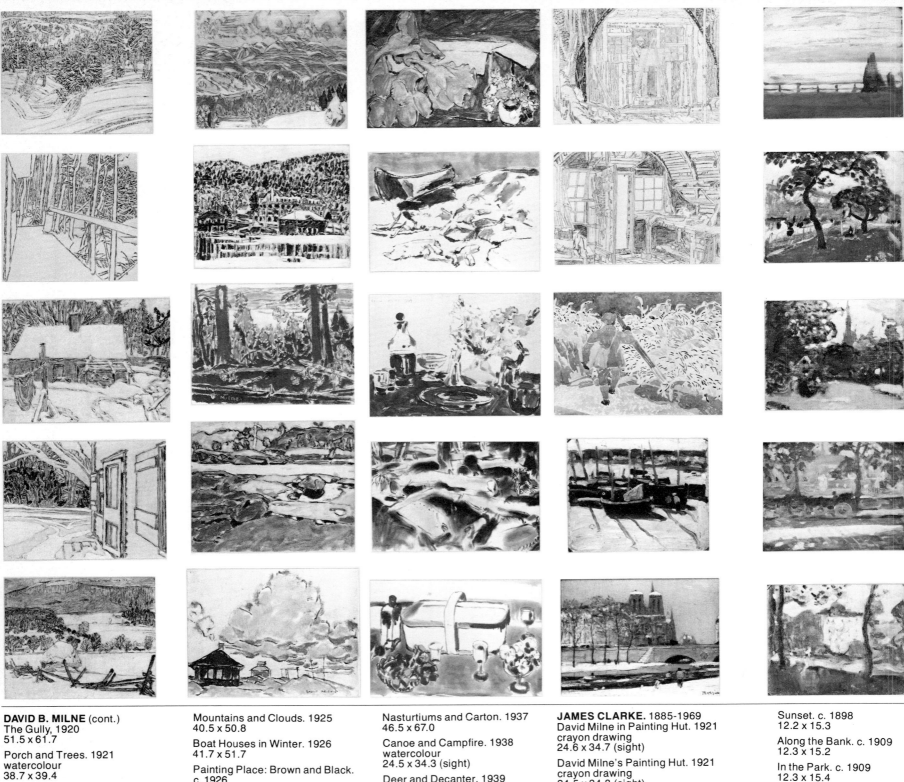

DAVID B. MILNE (cont.)
The Gully, 1920
51.5 x 61.7

Porch and Trees. 1921
watercolour
38.7 x 39.4

Clarke's House. 1923
30.8 x 40.8

Clarke's House. 1923
30.5 x 40.6

Haystack. 1923
41.2 x 51.2

Mountains and Clouds. 1925
40.5 x 50.8

Boat Houses in Winter. 1926
41.7 x 51.7

Painting Place: Brown and Black.
c. 1926
31.0 x 41.2

The Stream. c. 1928
45.7 x 56.0

Railway Station. c. 1929
30.9 x 41.0

Nasturtiums and Carton. 1937
46.5 x 67.0

Canoe and Campfire. 1938
watercolour
24.5 x 34.3 (sight)

Deer and Decanter. 1939
watercolour
35.0 x 48.3 (sight)

Forest Floor. c. 1943
watercolour
35.3 x 52.3

Pansies and Basket. c. 1947
watercolour
36.9 x 54.1

JAMES CLARKE. 1885-1969
David Milne in Painting Hut. 1921
crayon drawing
24.6 x 34.7 (sight)

David Milne's Painting Hut. 1921
crayon drawing
24.5 x 34.8 (sight)

David Milne on Painting Hike. 1921
watercolour
21.8 x 30.0 (sight)

J. W. MORRICE. 1865-1924
Harbour. c. 1898
12.7 x 15.3

Notre Dame, Paris. c. 1898
19.0 x 25.4

Sunset. c. 1898
12.2 x 15.3

Along the Bank. c. 1909
12.3 x 15.2

In the Park. c. 1909
12.3 x 15.4

Paris. c. 1909
12.3 x 15.3

Reflections. c. 1909
12.3 x 15.3

J. W. MORRICE (cont.)

The Promenade. c. 1909
12.3 x 15.3

Winter in France. c. 1909
12.3 x 15.4

Roadside Scene. c. 1911
12.2 x 15.3

Sailboat. c. 1911
12.4 x 15.3

Low Tide and Evening Clouds,
Brittany. 1912
17.8 x 25.2

Clam Digging, France. c. 1914
12.2 x 15.4

Kingston, Jamaica. 1915
pencil & wash
25.1 x 31.7

The Jetty. c. 1918
12.4 x 15.3

Village Square. c. 1918
12.1 x 15.3

Algiers. c. 1919
25.0 x 23.5

Tunis. c. 1920
watercolour
23.5 x 32.5

Landscape in Trinidad. c. 1921
38.0 x 46.6

ALBERT ROBINSON. 1881-1956

Nude. 1906
pencil
30.5 x 23.5

Scene in Laurentians. 1914
21.6 x 26.7

Quebec Houses and Yards. c. 1920
21.2 x 26.6

On the St. Lawrence. c. 1921
21.0 x 26.7

St. Joseph. 1922
70.0 x 85.1

Afternoon, St. Siméon. c. 1924
56.0 x 66.5

Gaspé Church. 1929
56.3 x 66.5

Haytime, Knowlton, Quebec.
c. 1930
56.7 x 67.0

TOM THOMSON. 1877-1917

Nearing the End. c. 1905
watercolour
34.9 x 56.8

Young Fisherman. c. 1905
pen and ink
31.3 x 47.0

Lady in Her Garden. 1906
46.0 x 25.4

Head of a Woman. 1907
watercolour
32.2 x 23.1

Sailboat. c. 1908
11.4 x 13.8

TOM THOMSON (cont.)
Burns' Blessing. 1909
watercolour
34.9 x 24.1

Sailboat. c. 1909
watercolour
15.6 x 22.6

Fairy Lake. 1910
17.7 x 27.7

A Northern Lake. c. 1913
17.5 x 25.2

Red Forest. 1913
17.2 x 25.1

Springtime, Algonquin Park. 1913
17.5 x 25.0

Pine Stump and Rocks. 1913
17.2 x 24.8

Sunset Over Hills. 1913
17.8 x 22.8

Abandoned Logs. 1914
21.6 x 26.6

Burned Over Land. 1914
21.2 x 26.7

Georgian Bay. 1914
21.6 x 26.7

Georgian Bay Islands #1. 1914
21.6 x 26.7

Georgian Bay Islands with Pine #2.
1914
21.6 x 26.7

New Life After Fire. 1914
21.5 x 26.7

Pine Island. 1914
21.7 x 26.7

Silver Birches. 1914
41.0 x 56.3

Spring. 1914
22.2 x 26.7

Twisted Maple. 1914
26.7 x 21.0

Afternoon, Algonquin Park. 1915
64.2 x 81.7

Algonquin, October. 1915
21.6 x 26.8

Autumn, Algonquin Park. 1915
51.8 x 41.9

Aura Lee Lake. 1915
21.3 x 26.7

Autumn, Algonquin. 1915
21.6 x 26.7

Autumn Clouds. 1915
21.8 x 26.7

Backwater. 1915
21.5 x 26.7

TOM THOMSON (cont.)

Burned Over Swamp. 1915
21.6 x 26.7

Dappled Thicket. 1915
21.6 x 26.7

Deer. 1915
Pencil
12.0 x 19.0

Deer. 1915
Pencil
12.0 x 19.0

Deer. 1915
Pencil
12.0 x 19.0

Evening Clouds. 1915
21.5 x 26.6

Hoar Frost. 1915
21.6 x 26.7

Islands, Canoe Lake. 1915
21.2 x 26.7

Late Autumn. 1915
26.7 x 21.6

Log Jam. 1915
12.6 x 17.5

Moonlight, Canoe Lake. 1915
21.9 x 26.7

Pine Cleft Rocks. 1915
21.3 x 27.7

Poplar Hillside. 1915
21.5 x 26.7

Rushing Stream. 1915
21.4 x 26.7

Smoke Lake. 1915
21.5 x 26.9

Snow Shadows. 1915
21.2 x 26.7

Spring Breakup. 1915
21.6 x 26.7

Spring Flood. 1915
21.2 x 26.7

The Clearing. 1915
26.7 x 21.6

The Log Flume. 1915
21.5 x 26.7

Beech Grove. c. 1915
21.7 x 26.5

Lake, Hills and Sky. c. 1915
21.4 x 26.7

Phantom Tent. c. 1915
21.4 x 26.7

Summer Day. c. 1915
21.6 x 26.8

Sunset. c. 1915
21.3 x 26.7

TOM THOMSON (cont.)
Wood Interior. c. 1915
21.5 x 26.8

Autumn Woods. c. 1915
21.6 x 26.7

Wood Interior, Winter. c. 1915
21.9 x 26.7

Autumn Birches. 1916
21.6 x 26.7

Autumn Colour. 1916
21.3 x 26.7

Black Spruce in Autumn. 1916
21.5 x 26.8

Purple Hill. 1916
21.5 x 26.7

Ragged Pine. 1916
21.5 x 26.6

Rocks and Deep water. 1916
21.0 x 26.7

Snow in the Woods. 1916
21.7 x 27.2

Sombre Day. 1916
21.5 x 26.7

Tamaracks. 1916
21.4 x 26.8

Tea Lake Dam. 1916
21.4 x 26.3

Algonquin Waterfall. c. 1916
21.2 x 26.7

Early Spring. c. 1916
21.6 x 26.7

Woodland Waterfall. 1916
123.0 x 132.5

Moonlight and Birches. c. 1916
22.0 x 27.0

Sunrise. c. 1916
21.6 x 26.7

Water Flowers. 1916
21.3 x 26.7

Summer Shore, Georgian Bay.
c. 1916
72.5 x 77.5

Windy Day. c. 1916
21.5 x 26.6

Widlflowers. 1917
21.7 x 26.8

F. H. VARLEY. 1881-1969
Indians Crossing Georgian Ba
1920
30.5 x 40.6

Stormy Weather, Georgian Ba
1920
21.6 x 26.7

Nude. c. 1920
62.0 x 51.5

F. H. VARLEY (cont.)
Little Girl. 1923
mixed media
36.7 x 28.7

Meadowvale. 1923
21.2 x 25.4

John in the Studio. 1924
pen and ink
27.5 x 22.0 (sight)

Mountain Portage. 1925
50.8 x 60.9

Girl in Red. 1926
53.5 x 52.0

Portrait of Old Man. c. 1926
charcoal
69.5 x 45.6

Mountains. 1927
pen and ink
30.3 x 35.4 (sight)

Sketchers. 1927
pencil
30.8 x 37.7 (sight)

Indian Girl. 1927
mixed media
22.3 x 19.9

Dead Tree, Garibaldi Park. c. 1928
30.4 x 38.0

Vera. c. 1928
31.7 x 34.3

Blue Pool. 1930
27.9 x 33.0

Sphinx Glacier, Mt. Garibaldi.
c. 1930
119.7 x 140.0

The Lions. c. 1931
30.5 x 38.1

Moonlight at Lynn. 1933
59.7 x 75.6

West Coast Inlet. c. 1933
30.5 x 38.0

Trees Against the Sky. 1934
30.4 x 38.3

Arctic Waste. 1938
watercolour
22.1 x 30.3 (sight)

Eskimo Woman. 1938
mixed media
22.8 x 8.7

Iceberg. 1938
30.4 x 38.0

Negro Head. 1940
40.2 x 30.6

Portrait of Dr. A. Mason. c. 1940
mixed media
35.4 x 25.2 (sight)

Fall Landscape. 1948
30.5 x 38.1

F. H. VARLEY (cont.)
Hilltop, Doon. 1948
30.0 x 38.2

Portrait of a Man. 1950
69.5 x 45.6

Little Lake, Bras d'Or. 1953
23.7 x 30.2

Pine Tree. c. 1959
mixed media
30.2 x 22.6 (sight)

ESKIMO SCULPTURE —All Eskimo sculptures are stone unless otherwise noted.

Enoogoo
Arctic Bay
stone/ivory 17.5 x 11.0 x 16.8

Samon
Arctic Bay
whalebone/sinew 11.7 x 19.2 x 6.6

Barnabas Akkanarshook
Baker Lake 28.0 x 45.0 x 35.0

Angrnasungaaq
Baker Lake 30.0 x 49.0 x 20.0

Aqiggaaq
Baker Lake 25.0 x 26.5 x 33.0

Eqilaq
Belcher Island, N.W.T.
39.0 x 23.0 x 23.7

Eegyvudluk
Cape Dorset
23.6 x 22.8 x 10.3

Kiawak
Cape Dorset
34.0 x 50.0 x 20.8

Mungita
Cape Dorset
35.3 x 34.3 x 14.0

Numani
Cape Dorset
51.8 x 32.2 x 28.0

Oshooweetook ''B''
Cape Dorset
86.5 x 32.0 x 28.0

Pauta
Cape Dorset
153.0 x 170.0 x 168.0

Pauta
Cape Dorset
58.8 x 27.3 x 23.3

Tukee
Cape Dorset
26.0 x 26.7 x 18.6

Artist unknown
Eskimo Point
14.5 x 8.7 x 11.3

Henry Naparpuk
Great Whale River
3.0 x 11.2 x 2.0

Davidee
Lake Harbour
40.5 x 17.0 x 25.5

Leah Eevik
Pangnirtung
multiple media
43.0 x 23.0 x 22.0

200

ESKIMO SCULPTURE (cont.)

Akulik
Port Harrison
27.9 x 48.6 x 19.1

Akulik
Port Harrison
54.0 x 26.2 x 17.5

Anowtuk
Povungnituk
56.3 x 44.3 x 42.7

Levi Qumaluk
Povungnituk
41.5 x 48.3 x 21.5

Levi Qumaluk. 1976
Povungnituk
34.2 x 37.5 x 22.0

Tiktak
Rankin Inlet
30.0 x 16.5 x 13.5

Alice Utakrala
Repluse Bay
14.3 x 4.4 x 6.5

Artist unknown
5.2 x 17.0 x 3.7

Artist unknown
antler
6.2 x 13.3 x 6.7

Henry
19.0 x 16.5 x 13.0

Artist unknown
27.4 x 19.8 x 5.5

Wall Hanging Oonark
Baker Lake wool
120.0 x 129.0

Food for my Children Tonight.
1975
Olassie Akulukjuk
Pangnirtung wool
140.4 x 87.8

ESKIMO PRINTS –

All Eskimo prints are stone
cuts unless otherwise noted.

Musk Ox Eating Grass. 1973
Anguhadluq/Tookoome   Baker Lake
stone cut/stencil 55.7 x 82.5 (sight)

Wolf Man. 1970
W. Noah/Oosuak/M. Noah
Baker Lake
stone cut/stencil 67.4 x 52.0 (sight)

Great Bull Caribou. 1972
W. Noah   Baker Lake
stone cut/stencil 59.4 x 99.9 (sight)

Big Woman. 1974
Oonark/Tookoome   Baker Lake
stone cut/stencil 50.6 x 68.3 (sight)

Musk Ox. 1971
Tookoome   Baker Lake
stone cut/stencil 58.9 x 81.0 (sight)

I am Always Thinking About the
Animals. 1974
Tookoome   Baker Lake
stone cut/stencil 54.4 x 78.5

Composition. 1967
Anirnik   Cape Dorset
40.9 x 58.2 (sight)

Woman with Water Pail. 1965
Eleeshushe   Cape Dorset
55.5 x 40.2 (sight)

Mountain Spirit. 1969
Johnniebo   Cape Dorset
57.5 x 73.5 (sight)

Summer Owl. 1971   Cape Dorset
Kananginak
72.2 x 56.3 (sight)

201

Nesting Bird. 1972 Kananginak Cape Dorset 55.3 x 75.9 (sight)	Strange Scene. 1964 Kaikshuk Cape Dorset 55.4 x 70.8 (sight)	Our Camp. 1974 Pitseolak Cape Dorset 72.8 x 57.6 (sight)

Nesting Bird. 1972
Kananginak   Cape Dorset
55.3 x 75.9 (sight)

Owl of Kingait. 1973
Kananginak   Cape Dorset
64.4 x 59.5 (Sight)

Umingmuk. 1973
Kananginak   Cape Dorset
58.0 x 78.3 (sight)

Woman in the Sun. 1960
Kenojuak   Cape Dorset
artist's proof 49.3 x 65.4

Young Girl's Thoughts of Birds. 1974
Kenojuak   Cape Dorset
55.0 x 74.6 (sight)

Strange Scene. 1964
Kaikshuk   Cape Dorset
55.4 x 70.8 (sight)

Man Hunting at Seal Hole. 1959
Niviaksiak   Cape Dorset
skin stencil 59.7 x 44.8 (sight)

The Hunters. 1962
Parr/Iyola   Cape Dorset
74.0 x 53.0

Tripto Toodja. 1973
Pitseolak   Cape Dorset
53.7 x 80.7 (sight)

Netsilik River. 1973
Pitseolak   Cape Dorset
78.5 x 60.0 (sight)

Our Camp. 1974
Pitseolak   Cape Dorset
72.8 x 57.6 (sight)

Summer Birds. 1974
Pitseolak   Cape Dorset
stone cut/stencil 59.0 x 40.0 (sight)

Female Eiders Frightened. 1960
Tikitok   Cape Dorset
skin stencil 42.9 x 64.6 (sight)

Crow and His Wife Agnaklu. 1974
L. Pitsiulak/I. Karpik   Pangnirtung
54.3 x 70.6 (sight)

Lumak. 1965
Davidialuk   Povungnituk
55.9 x 64.4

WEST COAST INDIAN ART —
All these carvings are in argillite by Haida Indians unless otherwise noted.

Issac Chapman
14.4 x 3.4 x 3.6

Isaac Chapman
15.5 x 3.4 x 3.9

Isaac Chapman
12.7 x 3.0 x 3.3

Isaac Chapman
15.9 x 3.6 x 3.5

Patrick Dixon
26.2 x 5.8 x 6.2

Patrick Dixon
21.3 x 6.0 x 6.2

Charles Edensaw
11.0 x 3.6 x 4.0

Charles Edensaw
16.4 x 3.5 x 3.0

Charles Edensaw
16.5 x 3.4 x 4.6

Charles Edensaw
mountain sheep horn.
c. 1890
32.5 x 5.5 x 3.4

Rufus Moody
12.6 x 3.8 x 4.7

Artist unknown
26.7 x 7.1 x 6.2

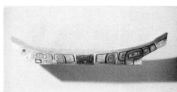

WEST COAST INDIAN ART (cont.)

Artist unknown
26.6 x 4.8 x 5.0

Artist unknown
34.9 x 6.8 x 5.6

Artist unknown
42.0 x 8.2 x 7.2

Artist unknown
40.3 x 8.1 x 8.2

Kwakiutl
Charlie James
wood/paint
49.7 x 28.5 x 12.5

Kwakiutl
Willie Seaweed
wood/paint
650.0 x 43.0 x 36.0

Kwakiutl House Post
Artist unknown
wood/paint
420.0 x 85.0 x 85.0

Female Figure
Artist Unknown
21.7 x 5.8 x 6.5

Dish
Patrick Dixon
2.8 x 10.0 x 4.6

Dish
Patrick Dixon
21.8 x 14.3 x 1.4

Dish
Tom Price
15.7 x 27.4 x 2.9

Killer Whale and Canoe
Henry White
15.5 x 19.1 x 6.8

Brown Salmon
Artist unknown
5.3 x 10.2 x 3.8

Pipe. c. 1875   Artist unknown
6.7 x 21.5 x 2.0

Pipe   Artist unknown
6.9 x 21.5 x 2.6

Nootka – Vase   Nootka – Paddle
Artist unknown   Artist unknown
cedar root   wood/paint
33.0 x 10.0 x 10.0   165.3 x 19.0

Tribe unknown
Model War Canoe. c. 1860
wood/paint 10.5 x 105.7 x 21.7

Tribe unknown
Fish Killing Club. c. 1860
wood 7.5 x 58.7 x 4.5

All West Coast Indian masks are wood and paint, and artist unknown unless otherwise noted.

Bella Bella Raven Mask.
c. 1870
19.0 x 23.5 x 41.5

Bella Bella Human Face Mask.
c. 1890   30.9 x 26.9 x 12.5

Bella Bella Human Face Mask.
c. 1890   28.5 x 21.0 x 13.5

Bella Bella Atlakim Mask.
c. 1900
33.7 x 20.1 x 14.0

Bella Coola Thunderbird Mask
32.5 x 25.5 x 26.4

Bella Coola Human Face Mask
25.2 x 28.3 x 12.0

Haida Portrait Mask:
Old Lady Wearing Labrette
23.6 x 18.4 x 11.4

Kwakiutl Atlakim Whale Mask.
c. 1902
Mungo Martin   multiple media
48.6 x 23.8 x 42.3

Kwakiutl Atlakim Salmon Mask
Mungo Martin
40.2 x 20.9 x 38.2

Kwakiutl Humanoid Mask
Mungo Martin   multiple media
36.7 x 29.0 x 14.8

203

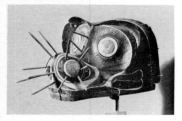

Kwakiutl Kingfisher Mask
attrib. to Mungo Martin   multiple media
20.3 x 21.0 x 28.2

Kwakiutl Frog Mask
attrib. to Mungo Martin   multiple media
31.2 x 28.5 x 45.4

Kwakiutl Wren Mask
attrib. to Mungo Martin   18.3 x 15.0 x 20.5

Kwakiutl Komokwa Mask with Fish. c. 1890
66.0 x 35.5 x 62.0

Kwakiutl Bumblebee Mask. c. 1900
multiple media   21.3 x 26.0 x 45.5

Kwakiutl Raven Hamatsa Mask
multiple media
23.2 x 22.5 x 109.0

Kwakiutl Crooked Beak of the Sky
Mask. c. 1880
multiple media
29.0 x 20.3 x 86.0

Kwakiutl Thunderbird Mask. c. 1943
multiple media
53.8 x 32.5 x 32.5

Kwakiutl Komokwa Mask
41.5 x 47.5 x 24.0

Kwakiutl Tsonaqua Masquette.
c. 1900
16.7 x 11.2 x 6.6

Nootka Face Mask. c. 1880
26.0 x 17.2 x 15.0

Nootka Face Mask. c. 1890
25.5 x 9.2 x 12.5

Nootka Face Mask
22.2 x 16.8 x 13.5

Salish (Swaixwe) Mask. c. 1870
76.2 x 32.0 x 24.5

Tlingit Wolf Masquette. c. 1860
12.5 x 8.3 x 7.0

Tsimshian Human Face Mask
22.0 x 16.8 x 12.8

Tsimshian Gurhsan the Gambler
Mask
25.5 x 16.5 x 8.2

Tsimshian Human Face Mask
23.1 x 18.3 x 7.9

Wolf Mask. c. 1870
multiple media
26.0 x 14.9 x 18.5

Raven Mask. c. 1870
25.5 x 9.9 x 8.6

Tsimshian Ceremonial Frontlet.
pre-1850
multiple media
17.5 x 14.6 x 5.2

Bella Coola Sisaok Frontlet. 1924
multiple media
54.0 x 31.5 x 38.0

Haida Raven Rattle. c. 1825
11.0 x 31.7 x 10.3

Kwakiutl Moon Rattle
33.2 x 18.0 x 12.7

Whale Rattle. c. 1870
28.9 x 10.8 x 13.0

204

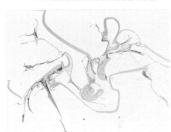

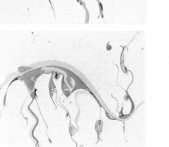

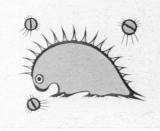

WEST COAST INDIAN ART (cont.)

Tsimshian Spoon. c. 1860
horn/argillite 6.5 x 29.5

Spoon
horn/argillite 29.3 x 6.5

Spoon
horn/argillite 18.2 x 5.5

Haida Spoon   Robert Davidson
silver 12.0 x 3.6

Copper
copper 22.7 x 12.9

Haida Bracelet. c. 1899
Charles Edensaw
gold 1.3 x 16.0 (circumference)

Haida Bracelet. c. 1910
Charles Edensaw
silver 6.4 x 19.9 (circumference)

Haida Bracelet. 1956   Bill Reid
silver (dia.) 6.4 x 4.5

WOODLAND INDIAN ART —

Demon Woman. 1975
Samuel Ashe
acrylic on art board   50.8 x 37.5

Protection. 1975
Jackson Beardy
acrylic on paper   30.0 x 40.0

Communication. 1975
Jackson Beardy
acrylic on paper   38.0 x 46.3

All Woodland Indian paintings are acrylic on canvas unless otherwise noted.

Moose. 1974
Benjamin Chee Chee
ink on paper 35.6 x 45.7

Bird with Antlers. 1974
Benjamin Chee Chee
ink/acrylic on paper 45.7 x 60.9

Dancing Goose. 1975
Benjamin Chee Chee
stencil on paper 60.9 x 76.2

Dancing Geese. 1975
Benjamin Chee Chee
stencil on paper 60.9 x 76.2

Bird and Friend. 1972
Blake Debassige 71.1 x 60.9

The Great and Mischievous
Nanabush. 1975   Blake Debassige
121.5 x 132.3

Dependency. 1978
Blake Debassige
101.5 x 76.4

The Bureaucratic Supremist. 1975
Alex Janvier
56.0 x 71.3

This Soil is Spirit. 1975
Alex Janvier
60.7 x 76.0

The Doggone Weakbacks. 1975
Alex Janvier
56.0 x 71.3

The Hunter Confronting the Bear
While the Raven Flies By. 1973
Francis Kagige
46.0 x 61.0

Migration. 1974   Francis Kagige
61.0 x 76.0

Why the Porcupine has Quills. 1975
Francis Kagige
61.0 x 76.0

The Owls. 1974   Goyce Kakegamic
acrylic on paper 62.9 x 88.9

They Found Him in the Broken Bark
Wigwam. 1975   Goyce Kakegamic
acrylic on paper 57.4 x 72.4

WOODLAND INDIAN ART (cont.)
Mide Ceremony. 1975
Joshim Kakegamic
acrylic on board
102.0 x 81.5

Windego Spirit. 1975
Joshim Kakegamic
acrylic on paper
105.0 x 75.5

Blue Indian Thinking. 1975
Clifford Maracle
122.1 x 122.1

Pageant Ponies. 1976
Clifford Maracle
152.1 x 122.0

Ghost Dancer. 1976
Clifford Maracle
60.7 x 60.6

Expectant Indian Woman. 1975
Johnson Meekis
91.5 x 61.1

My Grandfather. 1975
Johnson Meekis
60.9 x 91.5

Hunter. c. 1968
Norval Morrisseau
acrylic on board
108.5 x 69.5

Sacred Trout with Eggs. 1970
Norval Morrisseau
76.2 x 101.5

Artist Talks to the Bird's Form. 1975
Norval Morrisseau
76.2 x 101.6

Sacred Mide Bear and Loon Totem.
1975
Norval Morrisseau
76.2 x 101.5

Artist's Wife and Daughter. 1975
Norval Morrisseau
acrylic on masonite
101.6 x 81.3

Self-Portrait. 1975
Norval Morrisseau
acrylic on masonite
101.6 x 81.3

Artist's Three Sons. 1975
Norval Morrisseau
101.5 x 76.3

Tribute to the Great Chiefs of the
Past. 1975
Daphne Odjig
101.8 x 81.0

Conflict Between Good and Evil.
1975
Daphne Odjig
81.0 x 101.4

The Embrace. 1975
Daphne Odjig
101.4 x 80.8

The Guardian Spirit. 1974
Martin Panamick
76.4 x 61.0

Eagle. 1975
Martin Panamick
76.5 x 61.3

The Re-Creation of the World Aft
the Great Flood. 1975
Carl Ray
76.2 x 60.9

Drummer. 1975
Carl Ray
61.5 x 76.8

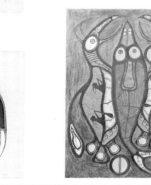

WOODLAND INDIAN ART (cont.)

Man Trying to Reach Heaven. 1975
Carl Ray
76.5 x 102.3

Frolicking Loons. 1975   Carl Ray
ink/acrylic on paper 55.9 x 76.2

Bang-Wa-Jusk the Man-Eater of the
Underworld. 1975   Carl Ray
ink/acrylic on paper 55.9 x 76.2

Conflict Between Good and Evil.
1975   Carl Ray
acrylic on paper 55.9 x 74.9

Old Mike. 1974   Arthur Shilling
acrylic on masonite 75.8 x 60.5

Jeannie. 1975
Arthur Shilling
oil on masonite
75.5 x 66.0

Self-Portrait. 1975
Arthur Shilling
oil on masonite
84.0 x 61.4

Thunderbird. 1975
James Simon
96.4 x 110.6

Thunderer Spirit. 1975
James Simon
76.0 x 91.3

Thunderbird, Demon Fish, Lightning
Snake. 1974
Roy Thomas
56.0 x 84.0

Thunderbird and Young. 1975
Roy Thomas
113.0 x 119.5

The Power of the Thunderbirds.
1978
Randy Trudeau
90.9 x 60.2

Thunderbirds and Sturgeons. 1975
Saul Williams
acrylic on paper
76.0 x 50.6

Wa-Pa-See. (Swan). 1975
Saul Williams
ink on paper
38.0 x 56.0

Windego Spirit. 1975
Saul Williams
acrylic on paper
61.0 x 48.0

Eagle Dancer Doll. 1975
Isobell Skye
multiple media
51.5 x 84.0 x 29.0

Mask. 1975   Beulah Nanticoke
corn husk 36.5 x 33.0 x 21.0

Blower Mouth Mask. 1975
Jacob E. Thomas
multiple media
27.6 x 17.8 x 13.5

Broken Nose Mask. 1975
Jacob E. Thomas
multiple media
26.5 x 17.2 x 13.8

Door Keeper Mask. 1975
Jacob E. Thomas
multiple media 26.5 x 17.5 x 14.0

Broken Nose Mask. 1975
Jacob E. Thomas
multiple media 27.0 x 23.0 x 12.5

207

WOODLAND INDIAN ART (cont.)
Iroquois Beadwork Pot. 1977
Sara Smith
clay 26.9 x 17.3 (diameter)
Moose Design Quill Box. 1977
Frances Abitong
multiple media
7.9 x 26.2 (diameter)
Symbolic Sculpture. 1975
Elwood L. Green
silver/stone 7.4 x 11.3 (diameter)
The Legend of the Crystal Bear.
1972   Joseph R. Jacobs
stone/abalone shell
25.7 x 21.5 x 28.2

The Seven Dancers. 1976
Joseph R. Jacobs
stone/ivory
39.0 x 30.0 x 32.2
Acceptance of Chief's Hat. c. 1977
Joseph R. Jacobs
multiple media
20.2 x 14.8 x 21.0
The Creation Legend. 1972
Duffy Wilson
stone
13.0 x 26.2 x 40.2
To do da ho. 1975
Duffy Wilson
stone
14.0 x 19.5 x 11.0

208

ACKNOWLEDGEMENTS

Bernhard Cinader,   Woodland Indian A.
Paul Duval   Biographi
Dorothy Harley Eber   Inuit A
Howard B. Roloff   West Coast Indian A

A. J. Casson,   Desig
Joachim Gauthier,   Portraits of Artis
Hugh W. Thompson   Photograph
Sampson Matthews Limited, Toronto   Print

© 1979 McMichael Canadian Collection
ISBN 0-920658-01-6
Printed in Canada